Dear Jane Austen
A Heroine's Guide to Life and Love

By
Patrice Hannon

WYTHERNGATE PRESS
2005

2005 Wytherngate Press

Cover photograph courtesy of
Hantsweb Tourism Information Service
provided by the
Hampshire City Council www.hants.gov.uk

Cover design by
Brenda Nemeth

Author portrait by
Ricardo de Masi Photography

ISBN 0-9728530-3-X

Wytherngate Press website: Wytherngate.com

The principal text of this book was set in a digitized version of 10 point
Bookman Old Style. Titles appear in Edwardian Script.

Printed in the United States of America on acid-free paper

Hannon, Patrice.
    Dear Jane Austen: A Heroine's Guide to Life and Love/ Patrice Hannon.
    166 p.; 21 cm.
    ISBN 0-9728530-3-X
    1. Women – Conduct of life. 2. Women – Psychology. 3. Heroines in
    literature. I. Austen, Jane, 1775-1817. Pride and Prejudice.

158.1

In loving memory of my parents,
Joseph and Marie (Joy) Hannon

Acknowledgements

I would like to thank my family, my friends, and my students for the love and support they have given me since I started writing this book several years ago. I could not have succeeded without their enthusiasm, encouragement, and advice. I am also grateful to my wonderful publisher, Pamela. I can only hope my humble appreciation of Jane Austen's great art is evident in every word of this tribute.

Contents

*I have had a most rare vision. I have had a
dream, past the wit of man to say what
dream it was.*
                        —William Shakespeare,
                        A Midsummer Night's Dream

*No one who had ever seen Catherine Morland
in her infancy, would have supposed her born
to be an heroine.... But from fifteen to seventeen she was in training for a heroine....*
                        —Jane Austen,
                        Northanger Abbey

Preface

Who is there? Ah, Fanny, pray come in. Dear Fanny, you have not been to fetch our letters in this cold stormy rain? How very kind of you. We had it settled that you would arrive later with your father in a manner befitting the mistress of Godmersham and Chawton House. Sit there by the window. I give you strict orders to find in a minute that the sky is looking brighter, and that it will certainly be quite clear by midday. The coach will go by soon to give your teeth a good rattle. If you fly downstairs and out the front door at the first tremor, perhaps you will spy a pair of hobnailed boots hanging out one door as it passes, and so will you be charmingly diverted imagining what sort of hat hangs out the other. Never say you are not royally entertained at Grandmama's house. I promise I shall not be a moment finishing this list for the butcher. What say you, do you think a joint of mutton will please the company tomorrow night?

> *She gloried in being a sailor's wife, but she must pay the tax of quick alarm for belonging to that profession which is, if possible, more distinguished in its domestic virtues than in its national importance.*
> *Finis.*

There. Now, my dear niece, are all those letters really for me? On my desk, if you please. Yes, thank you, I am feeling much better. No, nothing at all. I am quite content. I promise to come down soon, and if the weather clears we shall at least take a turn about the garden. I wish to show you our splendid new rosebushes. Your Aunt Cassandra's mulberry trees? Well, I will not say they are dead, but I am afraid they are not alive. Until later, my love.

Now, if I can discover where I have put my letter-opener I shall see what tales of woe have been sent to me from the twenty-first century. This melancholy day will just suit their mood. Here it is. You see, I had put my huswife upon it. Let us begin.

Dear Jane Austen,

Help! I have reached the age where I won't tell my age and I will die if I don't land a husband soon. Why am I still single? I read every relationship book that comes down the pike, take every man-catching class offered in my town, watch all the dating experts on television and I still have a hard time meeting someone I don't mind being seen with and then when I finally do he always dumps me just when I think he might truly be The One. And I have a dozen friends with the same problem. How can I find the right man, someone rich and handsome and tall like Mr. Darcy? And then when I've found him, how can I make him propose to me even once, never mind twice the way Mr. Darcy did? Dear Jane, tell me before I give up on men completely and take the veil: how can I live happily ever after like Elizabeth Bennet?

Wish I Were a Heroine

I must mend my pen and answer this sad girl without loss of time. I see I shall not be long in seeking occupation now I have said farewell to The Elliots.

Dear Would-be Heroine,

Your letter reveals the unfortunate influence of a culture distinguished by nothing so much as vulgarity and self-absorption. Yes, I have been studying your society for some time and am well acquainted with its absurdities. As a friend I would urge you to strive for some measure of self-command. Indeed, your hysterical raving would not be amiss in a Gothic novel, or something by one of those Brontës who, after all my labour to entertain women with sparkling comedies having only genius, wit, and taste to recommend them, set the poor creatures back hundreds of years with stories full of improbable circumstances and unnatural characters. These novels are fine entertainment, not unlike the sort my Catherine adored, but it is not in them that human nature is to be found. Catherine discovered that General Tilney had neither poisoned his wife nor imprisoned her deep in the recesses of Northanger Abbey, and unless it is your custom to form attachments with men who do such things—or who walk the moors in the moonlight with the ghosts of lovers twenty years dead as Heathcliff does—you should not look to such books—or their present-day descendants, Hollywood romances—for pictures of real men and women. Nor is that newer medium, television, which I understand has largely taken the place of books and plays as the entertainment of an evening, to be trusted. For despite its name, "reality television" puts men and women in situations equally unnatural and if, as is most likely, you are unacquainted with members of your sex who dress like Carrie Bradshaw or establish intimacies with the frequency and insensibility of Samantha Jones, by all means be entertained by the behaviour of these fictional characters too, as Catherine is by the heroines of her beloved novels, but do not for a moment believe that such behaviour resembles that of flesh and blood women. No, dear Heroine, you cannot do better than my novels if you seek

stories in which the greatest powers of the mind are displayed, in which the most thorough knowledge of human nature, the happiest delineation of its varieties, the liveliest effusions of wit and humour are conveyed to the world in the best chosen language.

You aspire to the fate of my darling Lizzy, and that arouses my interest and pity. First of all, take heart: a woman's "years of danger," as I call them in *Persuasion* (the name by which you know the novel I have just completed), come much later than they did in my day and, indeed, will never come at all if you heed my words. So now, put aside your fantastic notions of how to live. If you would be a heroine like Elizabeth Bennet, you have only to read carefully my answers to you and your sisters in misery. These letters hold my advice as it is illustrated in my novels. In them you will find *A Heroine's Guide to Life and Love.*

Your very sincere friend,

Jane Austen

There, that should suffice. Still, it is not always easy to give guidance to heroines-in-training who have lost their way. It is often heavy work indeed to dislodge cherished notions such as this one:

> "...we always know when we are acting wrong, and with such a conviction I could have had no pleasure."

That is the voice of my Marianne in *Sense and Sensibility.* Would-be heroines also tend to believe as my Fanny Price does that:

> "We have all a better guide in ourselves, if we would attend to it, than any other person can be."

If these opinions are correct, there is no necessity for the enterprise upon which I embark. Fanny and Marianne are very different creatures, to be sure, yet here they voice a similar sentiment. But is what they pronounce with such assurance true? Are we indeed invariably our own best advisors? If we are allowed to test the precept in Marianne's own case, we shall see that it is clearly not true at the time she says it, in the middle of her ill-conceived love affair with Willoughby, when she has no idea how very bad—albeit pleasurable—her behaviour is. On the other hand, Fanny is almost always right in her judgments, and even her creator hesitates to contradict her. But does Henry Crawford, to whom Fanny speaks, also have an unerring internal guide? He subsequently runs off with the married Maria Bertram, whom he does not even love, thereby ultimately ruining the happiness of many people, including himself...

Goodness! How the thunder startles one. It is raining so furiously I fear there will not be a petal left alive. Well, there has been little of the summer in this July. It is a certainty that only a fervent romantic like Marianne could find the charm of the picturesque in such dreary skies. To continue, then:

Long habits of indulgence and self-created delusions erode the solidity and weaken the influence of such internal guides to conduct as we possess in ourselves if we were once taught good principles. I trust that my readers were so taught. I rely on their ability to recognize sound advice when they hear it, even if they have long been deaf to these inner voices of wisdom. In this, you already resemble my own darling girls, who are similarly deluded and must endure a painful awakening, a moment of enlightenment in which they see clearly their mistaken course of conduct. (We cannot say too little of Emma's internal guide until that moment of illumination, though she herself has the utmost faith in its reliability. In the twentieth century someone borrowed her story and called it *Clueless.*) With this book I hope to spare you the pain my girls endure but supply the same enlightenment. Not for all the world would I have you sleep in your errors even one night longer. In turn I hope you will thank me as Elizabeth Bennet thanked her aunt "for the kindness of her hints...a wonderful instance of advice being given...without being resented."

By the bye, I have recently made a survey of your circulating library, where I was astonished to find volumes containing enough conduct guides to stretch, if laid end to end, from Bath to Southampton. It is evident that my Emma is not the only clueless female. Some of these books contain quite good advice, while others are thoroughly nonsensical but I dare say my own novels, if read properly, will be your best guide. You must not confound my meaning, however: I did not write to instruct (or "to torment," which, as Catherine Morland reminds us, might sometimes be used synonymously with that verb). My stories are not moral lessons. Rather, I draw human nature with the aim of entertaining. Quite simply, as poor Virginia Woolf said of my characters, "People are like that..." (I shall never get over her drowning herself that way. We Austens have always faced adversity with a cooler gaze.) But in revealing true rather than wildly unnatural feelings and behaviour, I illustrate with great precision the most likely results of various choices and I leave it to you to deduce the wisdom and folly of the behaviour from the consequences. I give advice only where it is requested, and hope for no more praise as a counselor than is contained in Mrs. Smith's modest panegyric on Nurse Rooke in *Persuasion*:

> She is a shrewd, intelligent, sensible woman. Hers
> is a line for seeing human nature; and she has a fund
> of good sense and observation which, as a compan-
> ion, make her infinitely superior to thousands of
> those who having only received "the best education in
> the world," know nothing worth attending to.

So if you are casting about for the way to find happiness, read these letters. And then read my novels again, and you will find yourself in a fair way to becoming as much a heroine as my beloved children, Catherine, Elinor, Elizabeth, Fanny, Emma, Anne, and yes, even Marianne.

Ah, I see peeking out of the pile of letters Fanny has placed on my desk a lavender envelope. I suspect the writer to be a romantic. Upon closer inspection I see that the direction was written remarkably ill and then further obscured—no doubt by tears that fell upon it in torrents. I shall turn to this melancholy letter at once, as the lady appears to be in the greatest distress and in dire need of rational advice. Could my words flow as fast as the rain in the storecloset it would be charming.

Chapter One
A Heroine's Character

"Till this moment, I never knew myself."
—Elizabeth Bennet, *Pride and Prejudice*

Dear Jane Austen,

My love life is the pits. Everyone says I'm pretty and nice and smart but I can't hold on to a boyfriend. I am obsessed with the idea that if I were only taller, or thinner, or more athletic, or had thicker hair, or wore better clothes, or danced better...if I were just different—somehow better—I could keep a boyfriend. What do your heroines know that I don't know? How can I be perfect the way they are?

Hating Myself

~~&~~

Dear Hating Heroine,

Your mistake is one that millions of women fall into. In your distress you imagine my heroines to be without flaw but a moment's cooler reflection will show you your error. Pictures of perfection, like the heroines of romance novels, make me sick and wicked, and you will not find them in my books. I shall reserve my discussion of a heroine's positive attributes for another place in this chapter; you are rather in need of instruction regarding the all too evident faults my heroines display.

Perhaps you are thinking of the way women on Internet dating sites (extraordinary notion!) write of themselves: "Beautiful, brilliant, witty, athletic; the figure of a Victoria's Secret model, the voice of Renee Fleming; Anna Kournikova type, but better at tennis." This also seems to be the model for the women gentlemen are seeking there, if one can judge by the descriptions of their ideal mates. And you compare yourself to this paragon, a modern version of the "accomplished woman" Miss Bingley and Mr. Darcy discuss:

"A woman must have a thorough knowledge of music, singing, drawing, dancing, and the modern languages...and besides all this, she must possess a certain something in her air and manner of walking, the tone of her voice, her address and expressions, or the word will be but half deserved."

"All this she must possess," added Darcy, "and to all this she must yet add something more substantial, in the improvement of her mind by extensive reading."

But surely you did not put down *Pride and Prejudice* before hearing Elizabeth's reply to these self-serving remarks: "*I* never saw such a woman. *I* never saw such capacity, and taste, and application, and elegance, as you describe, united." No woman is without weaknesses and flaws. Elizabeth does not torment herself with invidious comparisons, although she knows very well that she is only moderately accomplished, her musical performance "by no means capital." And as for her looks, Mr. Darcy at first pronounces her "not handsome enough to tempt [*him*]." Her manners, moreover, are "not those of the fashionable world." Yet she has pride in herself, pride enough to refuse a most desirable marriage proposal when she is offended by the gentleman's behaviour and manner of address.

> **JANE AUSTEN SAYS: A HEROINE HAS PRIDE DESPITE HER IMPERFECTIONS.**

My father, you know, was a clergyman and wrote many a sermon on the subject of Pride. I am far from recommending that my heroines take as their ruling principle a Deadly Sin. But pride is a complicated matter, a word with more than one meaning, as that memorable discussion in *Pride and Prejudice*—surely you recall it—illustrates:

"Vanity and pride are different things, though the words are often used synonymously. A person may be proud without being vain. Pride relates more to our opinion of ourselves, vanity to what we would have others think of us."

You will recall that this is the voice of pompous, pedantic Mary. (Do not you love the way I slip something of real pertinence into her tired prosings? Harriet Smith, Mr. Woodhouse, Mrs. Bennet, Miss Bates—how often a home truth comes out of the mouths of those characters whose speech is otherwise largely nonsense!) I speak to you here of real pride, not mere vanity, although in my novels I too use the word "pride" at times to mean something less admirable than the trait I consider requisite for all heroines.

Emma Woodhouse, though she too is a delight, is also far from perfect, being proud and sometimes vain as well. You will recall that Mr. Knightley told Emma she saw in Jane Fairfax "the really accomplished young woman, which she wanted to be thought herself." And why is Emma not accomplished? Mr. Knightley again supplies the answer: "She will never submit to any thing requiring industry and patience, and a subjection of the fancy to the understanding." When one considers that Emma would not apply herself diligently to her lessons, her playing and drawing are not at all bad. Still, "...she was not unwilling to have others deceived, or sorry to know her reputation for accomplishment often higher than it deserved." Ah, there is Emma's vanity at work in her greater concern for her reputation than the actual level of her accomplishment. And yet, dear Hating

Heroine, can it admit of doubt which woman—Emma or Jane—is worthier to be preferred by the hero?

Young Catherine Morland similarly fails in becoming highly accomplished: "...she was often inattentive, and occasionally stupid" during her studies, showing no aptitude for either music or drawing. No, talents and accomplishments are not the measure of a heroine. And they are certainly not the means to captivate a hero, as my Lady Susan, middle-aged (for her era, though perhaps not yours) yet irresistible to men, knew very well: "...to be mistress of French, Italian, German, music, singing, drawing, etc., will gain a woman some applause, but will not add one lover to her list." Indeed, it is Catherine's eagerness to learn from Henry Tilney, not her accomplishments, that he finds irresistible. Her ignorance assures him that he has something valuable to offer her: he has a service to perform in her life.

Yes, but surely great physical beauty is necessary in a heroine, I hear you say. I could name many famous women who are reputed to be great beauties in your society, and yet if they are examined objectively, how many will, like Elizabeth, be seen to have "more than one failure of perfect symmetry in [their] form"? This one has no neck and, to put it as delicately as possible, an unusual and vulgar heaviness in a certain part of her figure, another has a large flat nose, another a diminutive stature, yet another the inelegant frame of a giantess. I shall devote a later chapter entirely to the discussion of the subject of beauty, but suffice it to say here that these flawed women simply do not let their imperfections erode their opinion of themselves and neither should you. They present themselves to the world with confidence—or at least the appearance of confidence—in their worthiness to be adored, and the world takes them at their word. For the next line of Lady Susan's letter quoted above is: "Grace and manner after all are of the greatest importance." And whence derive a heroine's grace and manner? Read my answer to the following query from your sister heroine and you will learn the answer.

Stay, I feel I must add a final note to this answer or risk leaving you in some confusion. Do not mistake me. I am certainly not encouraging ignorance. My heroines appreciated wit and accomplishment and despised ignorance. Dear Emma mightily wished she were more accomplished. Anne Elliot preferred the company and conversation of clever, talented people above all other. Although Catherine herself was ignorant and not at all witty, Henry Tilney's cleverness interested and amused her. Heroines should certainly strive to be accomplished, and, moreover, beautiful if they possibly can be. I merely point out that heroines should not suffer the least feelings of inadequacy if they are deficient in any of these areas except insofar as such feelings will spur them to make up the deficiencies. For it is not the deficiencies themselves but a heroine's belief in her unworthiness that will prevent her from attracting a hero or, indeed, achieving any ends she desires to achieve. Would I have become an authoress—and one not without admirers—if I had paused to compare my modest talent and education to those of the giants who strode before me—Fielding, Richardson, Smollett, Johnson, Burney, Radcliffe, and Edgeworth—and weighed my own worth on a scale against their undisputed excellence?

Believe me ever your faithful friend,

Jane Austen

> **JANE AUSTEN SAYS: BEAUTY, TALENT, LEARNING, AND ACCOMPLISHMENTS ARE NOT THE MEASURE OF A HEROINE.**

Dear Jane Austen,

I'm so confused. Do men like women who are quiet or talkative; outgoing or shy; friendly or aloof; smart or not so smart; responsible and thoughtful; or head-strong and bold? I get so many conflicting messages from so many experts that my head is spinning. I just don't know how to behave—or even how to be! Please help.

Bewildered

~~&~~

Dear Bewildered Heroine,

It is a source of some distress to me that young ladies should seek to regulate their conduct based upon what will attract members of the other sex rather than on what is good and right in itself. I beg you to recall that such women as do so in my novels are invariably disappointed. As Elizabeth says to Mr. Darcy when accounting for his initial interest in her:

"...you were sick of civility, of deference, of officious attention. You were disgusted with the women who were always speaking and looking, and thinking for *your* approbation alone. I roused, and interested you, because I was so unlike *them*...in your heart, you thoroughly despised the persons who so assiduously courted you."

Elizabeth is describing in particular her self-styled rival for Mr. Darcy's affection, Miss Bingley, whose behaviour is, however ineptly, entirely aimed at winning the gentleman's favour. Do not emulate her! Concentrate your attention rather on what excites, interests, educates, amuses, and improves *you*, without excessive concern for how your choice will be rated by men. I am not speaking of a civil agreeability regarding matters of little consequence but of the weak susceptibility to male opinion that exposes a deficient character.

You ask what type of woman you should be. You will notice that my heroines are quite different from one another. There is no single heroine *type* in my novels because my characters, unlike those in other

novels, are not puppets who display none of the
feelings, thoughts, or behaviour of real people. What
my heroines have in common, however, is a firm
character that does not bend with every male influence. (Nor are their spirits entirely at the mercy of the
amount of male attention they receive, something
that cannot be said of inferior characters. When the
regiment is about to leave Meryton, "...all the young
ladies in the neighbourhood were drooping apace. The
dejection was almost universal. The elder Miss Bennets alone were still able to eat, drink, and sleep, and
pursue the usual course of their employments.") Do
not mistake me. I am not praising a foolish inflexibil-
ity. Sooner or later—well, yes, later, to be sure—my
girls recognize their faults and acknowledge their
errors. They determine to change with the aim of
improving their thinking and behaviour but not in
order to please a man—although it sometimes happens that their change of behaviour *is* pleasing to
their heroes...

Ah, Cassandra, come in. You are quite right; I have let
our fire die down. My would-be heroines are such engross-
ing charges! Is not it a fine July when we need a fire while
the sun is up? Save your absent-minded sister from the ill
effects of her own blunder: pray, stir the fire.

You are always my most appreciative audience so I appeal to you, Cass, if what I have just told this poor bewildered child is not true. When sweet Emma realizes how
cruel she has been to Miss Bates, does she not seek to
make amends to the lady from the purest of motives? And is
not Mr. Knightley deeply moved by her selfless gesture? He
is also pleased by her improved opinion of Robert Martin,
but neither has she changed her view of that young farmer
merely to make him happy.

Well, Bewildered Heroine, I need not have feared a
blind partiality on the part of my sister! Cassandra,
with her starched notions, scolds me for being too
indulgent with Emma—an inclination she herself is
proof against. Indeed, I fear she does not like my
heroine much. Cass is taking up her copy of *Emma*

and—good heavens, she is reading to me from the scene where Emma leaves Hartfield and walks into Highbury intending to make amends to Miss Bates. I copy the significant line here verbatim so that you too may benefit from my sister's tutelage: "Her eyes were towards Donwell as she walked, but she saw him not." Well, perhaps the pure and impure motive are mingled even here. To be sure, it does appear now I hear it again that Emma's regard for Mr. Knightley is motivating her newfound solicitude for Miss Bates— or at least influencing it. Though I wrote the words myself I scarcely recalled that blemish. Well, my heroines are mixed characters, after all, neither angels nor fiends, and who could wish them otherwise? If they were not so true to life they would not serve as examples for the young women reading my words at this moment. And Emma's behaviour is so much the right thing here that one can hardly fault her for hoping her beloved observes it.

Yes, Cass, you are right; I do indulge her too much, like a naughty but irresistible child. I find her faultless in spite of all her faults, just as you find me.

There, I knew I would send her off with a shake of the head, a poke at the fire, and a smile.

Despite my formidable elder sister's correction, upon reflection, I do not change my views—but pray do not repeat that to her. Women who are too heavily influenced in their behaviour by men they are courting—a strange reversal!—surely have weak or corrupt characters. Like Mr. Frank Churchill, they are "not quite the thing." Miss Bingley provides an excellent example of such weakness, as I have said. She refuses to play cards because she has ascertained that Mr. Darcy does not want to, and she reads the second volume of a book—or pretends to—merely because Darcy is reading the first; she idiotically admires the speed of his writing and his penmanship; she will not join with Elizabeth in making fun of him, though in his impertinence he deserves to be mocked. This behaviour and her relentless jealousy of Elizabeth cause her to suffer a great deal. Who but herself is to blame for that suffering?

Isabella Thorpe, Catherine Morland's "dear friend," is another example of such a woman. She is entirely motivated by her fluctuating superficial desire for the attention of one man or another. She makes and breaks engagements, literally follows young men through the streets of Bath, and flirts most danger-ously and openly with Captain Tilney, a man who is not her betrothed. Eleanor Tilney is properly aston-ished at the suggestion that any man would admire "[a] girl who, before his eyes, is violating an engage-ment voluntarily entered into with another man." Captain Tilney's vanity is naturally flattered, and he carries on the flirtation for as long as it amuses him before dropping Isabella, leaving her not only sorely disappointed but publicly spurned and humiliated. Catherine is severe in her judgment of Tilney's easy manner: "But, suppose he had made her very much in love with him?" In response to which, Henry points out that Isabella's open lack of principle is precisely what allowed his brother's dismissive treatment. Had she herself been a different sort of girl "...she would have met with very different treatment." If a woman will offer herself as cheap and common, do not blame the gentleman for taking her at her word.

As a result of this susceptibility to the influence of men, Isabella ends up quite pathetic and miserable—again, a situation entirely of her own creation. The appearance of pride is, upon closer inspection, shown to be mere vanity as we—or, more accurately, Mary Bennet—make the distinction.

Maria and Julia Bertram of Mansfield Park, though their wealth and indulgent upbringing have certainly made them vain, are also without true pride or they would not repeatedly and eagerly bend to suit Henry Crawford's whims. Even without such pride, Maria should have been made proof against her ultimate degradation by a concern for the world's opinion of her, but her passion for a man who did not pay her the compliment of returning the feeling proved even stronger than her considerable vanity. Her sister Julia, though she is saved by luck from suffering such severe consequences, and displays a late-blooming concern with self-preservation, has not pride enough to prevent her from making a fool of herself over the same man.

Of all my heroines, Marianne is by far the least proud. She is early on influenced by love to mirror Willoughby's bad behaviour. Then, even after Willoughby has dismissed her with repeated insults, she continues to humiliate herself by pursuing him—without success. With the common perversity of the romantic, she actually boasts of her failing:

"No, no," cried Marianne, "misery such as mine has no pride. I care not who knows that I am wretched. The triumph of seeing me so may be open to all the world. Elinor, Elinor, they who suffer little may be proud and independent as they like—may resist insult, or return mortification—but I cannot."

This is a danger you must guard against, my readers, as the romantic influence is even stronger now than it was in Marianne's day and has many a would-be heroine bewildered: do not allow a lack of pride to appear in your own mind as a badge of honor in the deluded belief that it shows the depth and magnitude of your feeling, which "mere" pride cannot hold in check. This is a manifestation of a kind of perverse vanity, allowable only in women named Patsy or Dolly, who make their fortunes by *playing at* woeful desperation. In real life, passion unaccompanied by reason or self-respect is a black and miserable thing. And if self-respect is not an attractive enough end in itself, you will note that self-abasement has exactly the opposite effect from the desired one and does not secure for a heroine the hero for whom she has given up her dignity. A hero wants a truly proud woman who knows her own worth, and not a puppet or a slave. If she does not value herself, how can he value her? (And your era has discovered ingenious ways to multiply opportunities for self-humiliation. Were

Marianne living in your time she would not stop at "dialing while drunk" but would descend to the level of *bona fide* stalker, driving by Combe Magna and frequenting Willoughby's London haunts—though I assure you, his black pointer bitch would be quite safe from any unfortunate accidents at her hands, as her powerful destructive tendencies are all directed inward.)

Jane Fairfax, with all her superior gifts of notable beauty, good manners, and great musical talent, appears also to have pride yet she makes herself ill, physically and emotionally wretched, by acting "contrary to all [her] sense of right" at Frank Churchill's behest, agreeing to a secret engagement during which she is in "a state of perpetual suffering." In addition to the pain intrinsic to her position, she also endures repeated humiliation while her betrothed flirts outrageously with Emma in front of her—Emma, whose own pride would not allow her ever to act in the same way:

"And how could *she* bear such behaviour! Composure with a witness! to look on, while repeated attentions were offering to another woman, before her face, and not resent it. —That is a degree of placidity, which I can neither comprehend nor respect."

Only when Jane refuses to countenance further insult is the wedding date set.

And so you see, my Bewildered Heroine, how a lack of pride leads to behaviour that is bad on several counts. I do not like delivering sermons, and I know your age has far less use for moral law than even mine did, so we may leave morality aside in the question. A heroine is merely looking after her own best interests when she is firm in her own *good* judgment and does not allowed herself to be swayed from it by the deep desire for a hero's approbation.

Now, as Cass will quickly remind me, it is a fault to be too sure of one's *bad* judgment, as my heroines sometimes are. Elizabeth, Emma, Catherine, Marianne—all are guilty of this charge. Being real young women, not spotless angels, they are indeed flawed, and vanity is often a companion to pride. But it is far worse to move not of one's own will but merely in response to the pull of a larger body, upon whom one is entirely dependent for the determination of one's opinions and activity—in short, to be a satellite instead of a system. (I believe I am poaching that metaphor from another writer. Is it George Eliot? I cannot recollect. I use such tropes rarely. She has them to spare. A brilliant woman, to be sure, but her novels are rather uphill work, do not you think? And her poetry—good heavens!—it is not to be thought of!)

I remain yours very sincerely,

Jane Austen

JANE AUSTEN SAYS: A HEROINE IS NOT UNDULY INFLUENCED BY THE DESIRE TO SECURE A HERO'S APPROVAL.

Dear Jane Austen,

I think I will lose my mind if you can't help me. I am a very shy, nervous girl. I have so many phobias—fear of driving, of public speaking, of men. Even my shyness is a pathological fear: it is called "social phobia." Your heroines are all so outgoing—so witty and fearless. No wonder men love them! What hope is there for a wallflower like me?

Timid and Trembling

~~&~~

Dear Timid Heroine,

As I assured your sister, Bewildered Heroine, my heroines are by no means all alike. While it is true that Elizabeth Bennet, Emma Woodhouse, and Elinor Dashwood are witty and self-assured, you may take

some comfort in the fact that Fanny Price is very shy.
Anne Elliot is quiet and even low-spirited at times.
Catherine Morland, as I have said, is no wit; she is
very naïve and unsure of herself in Bath society. You
must be true to yourself and not attempt to be what it
is not in your nature to be...

Henry! You startle me. With so many brothers I should
be used to such mischievousness. You doubt me, Henry?

Ah, my brother says that I am not being honest,
that it is plain to see I prefer the clever girl—and
moreover, that my readers do too. An open temper
and a lively wit, he says, I must love above all others.
As proof he presents the case of Mary Crawford,
whom he calls the true heroine of *Mansfield Park.*
Heresy!

Yes, Henry, I know you like the Crawfords. You have told
me often enough.

Would you believe, Timid Heroine, that my whole
family united against me to approve of Mary and
dislike Fanny? My niece Anna, a prodigiously clever
girl herself—although I confess there often appears to
be something of madness in her—could not bear my
heroine, and my mother dared to declare her "in-
sipid." Meanwhile, everyone adored the witty, ironic,
open-tempered and—might I point out?—grossly
immoral Miss Crawford. That is deep and artful, to be
sure, to suggest that I do not know which is the
heroine of my own novel. I do not say that Mary is not
on the surface the more delightful of the two. Do you
think I did not know that I was making her irresistible? I merely caution that such powerful appeal can
be deceiving. In short, my dear Readers, by all means,
be witty if possible. But we all have natural tempera-
ments and if you are not witty and gregarious it does
no good for me to declare that you must be so against
your nature—indeed, against any possibility of your
being so! If you are quiet like Fanny then you cannot

pretend you are outgoing and lively. As far as that goes, you can, you need, only be yourself.

What's this? Henry is putting some of my own writing under my nose. He refuses to concede the point. It is my charming satire, "Plan of a Novel, According to Hints from Various Quarters." What line should I read, Henry? "Heroine a faultless Character herself—, perfectly good, with much tenderness & sentiment, & not the least Wit..." Ah, Henry proposes that if I describe my mock-heroine in that satirical way then I must in fact believe a model heroine possesses quite the opposite nature. Well, my dear brother is wrong, but I will grant him this: in addition to pride, my heroines do share another attribute that cannot be dismissed even if it is not part of a woman's natural tendencies. She must develop this trait as part of her heroine training. It is in a way related to pride, as it also has at its root a strong sense of self-worth. It is courage, and if, as you, my Timid Heroine, say, you have it not, you must cultivate it by acting as if you do. Take care—by courage I do not mean Marianne's reckless imprudence in her behaviour with Willoughby, nor Lydia Bennet's improper boldness, in every circumstance, with every body; I mean, rather, the courage to speak and act forthrightly when justice, goodness, pride, and proper self-interest demand it.

> **JANE AUSTEN SAYS: A HEROINE HAS THE COURAGE OF HER CONVICTIONS.**

While Lydia's recklessness is very bad—in your day she would no doubt be starring in *Girls Gone Wild* videos and exposing herself in exchange for gaudy trinkets during Mardi Gras festivities—her sister Kitty's fretful timidity is even less attractive. But how much more admirable than both is Elizabeth Bennet's courage in the face of every fearful situation, whether it be the three-miles' solitary journey to

Netherfield to attend her sick sister, the impertinent questioning of her by the imperious Lady Catherine de Bourgh, or the many encounters with Mr. Darcy before, during, and after Elizabeth's falling in love with him, when she speaks with more courage than any woman he has ever known—and thereby bewitches him. As she so nicely sums it up, "My courage always rises with every attempt to intimidate me."

Note in particular Elizabeth's "desperate resolution" to walk on alone with Mr. Darcy and thank him for his successful effort to discover the whereabouts of Lydia and Wickham, and to bring about their marriage. Sometimes a heroine must summon the courage to act in order to show a hero his attentions would welcome. She must be as willing to take this risk with a man who has already proved himself worthy—and who may be labouring under a misapprehension as to her feelings towards him—as she would risk losing any suitor who has not done so.

But not only self-assured heroines like Elizabeth show courage, and you need not necessarily be so bold as to find any dare irresistible, as she does. (Notice how she is immediately provoked to do the very thing Charlotte defies her to do.) You may respectably live up to the heroine ideal by limiting your acts of courage to situations of some consequence. Catherine Morland, though young and rather diffident, withstands the strenuous united efforts of her dearly beloved brother and best friend to persuade her to do what she knows is wrong. When she is nonetheless tricked into breaking an engagement with the Tilneys, she races to their lodgings and does not even wait to be admitted by the servant but bursts into the drawing room to explain the misunderstanding to the astonished family, including the fearsome General Tilney. Though her behaviour is not strictly within the bounds of propriety, it only increases her appeal to Henry.

Anne Elliot, though reserved and gentle by nature, takes charge after Louisa's accident at Lyme with such confidence that even the strong, robust gentlemen present look to her for direction. Later on, she boldly takes it upon herself to address Captain Wentworth when he arrives for the concert, causing him to stop and speak to her rather than pass on, and she speaks to him again in an explicit attempt to prevent his departure. When she fears he still misunderstands her feelings, on another occasion she speaks to Captain Harville in his hearing in order to give him a hint. Though her speech leaves her trembling, she will deliver it rather than chance the possibility of his continuing in error. And at the risk of saying something that will be transparent to those listening and thereby expose her, she makes sure it is understood that Captain Wentworth's presence is very much desired at her father's party. So, while the headstrong and heedless Louisa Musgrave appears on the surface to be the bolder woman, Anne's courage is equally great, and of a superior kind because directed towards superior ends.

Emma Watson shows little concern for the stares she risks when she dances with ten-year-old Charles Blake after Miss Osborne has broken her promise to be his partner (though in the event such observation rather distresses her): "...he stood the picture of disappointment, with crimsoned cheeks, quivering lips, and eyes bent on the floor...Emma did not think, or reflect; —she felt and acted." Intent on soothing a child's injured feelings, Emma is regardless of her own vanity. Her courageous, good-hearted action, in true heroine style, succeeds in restoring little Charles's joyous spirits.

And who braver than my other darling Emma, when she insists on hearing what Mr. Knightley wants to say to her, though she fears it is a confession of his love for Harriet Smith (a girl mortally afraid of a ragtag band of gypsy children!)?

Henry, you do not smile. My dear brother, why the serious face? You are thinking of Eliza now. Ah, who braver indeed? I am sorry. Your poor wife faced her trials with tremendous fortitude. A husband guillotined by a bloodthirsty mob, a sick child who died young, a beloved mother wasted by disease, a terrible, painful illness of her own. But let us not forget she was an Austen by birth as well as marriage, and had courage in her blood.

I think of my great-grandmother, Timid Heroine, who condescended to take a job as schoolmistress when she was left a widow and the promises of her father-in-law to be kind to her and her seven children were forgotten. Through hard work and determination she thereby saw all her children launched in the world before she died. Her actions were not those of a weak-spirited woman. No more were those of her grandchild, Aunt Phila—Eliza's mother—who announced at the age of twenty-one that she was off to India to seek her fortune. In conclusion, I urge you to follow the examples of these courageous women real and fictional, and show courage if you would be a heroine also.

Yours very faithfully,

Jane Austen

Think of it, Henry, a girl of that age going halfway around the world alone to a strange, wild country to find a husband. What is that? You bid me remember Aunt Jane? Well, she is a relation by marriage only but to be sure she showed great courage in her own way during that terrible ordeal in Bath. To think that our rich aunt was accused of shoplifting a bit of lace! Unimaginable—and so the jury thought in the end. But she had to endure such indignities! Seven months at the Ilchester prison keeper's house, where—did you know—Mama asked her if she would like Cassandra or me to keep her company. Yes, it is quite true. Thank goodness Aunt Jane refused. And then, imagine how she spoke in her own defense in front of a packed courtroom. Spoke very well, judging from the verdict. And Mama again tried to send us to her and she said a courtroom was no place for young ladies. Poor Aunt Jane. I have not always spoken kindly of her but she is not a bad soul. Indeed, I hope others will remember me kindly, and forget my own little irritating ways. I sometimes fear it will not be long before they are put to the test on the matter. And then I will have need of courage myself. Was I mumbling? I beg your pardon. Oh, nothing, nothing worth repeating, my brother. I merely said that I only hope my girls reflect the strain of courage in our bloodline in their own modest ways. Why, there's your sermon, ready made. I shall hear it thunder through church next Sunday. I have become solemn enough for the pulpit and so must lay down my pen forever.

Yes, I did shiver. How attentive you are. Would you be so kind as to put more wood on the fire? This is roughish weather for anyone in a tender state. Do you not feel an unpleasant chill in the air?

Chapter Two
A Heroine and Her Family

I leave it to be settled by whomsoever it may
concern, whether the tendency of this work
be altogether to recommend parental tyranny,
or reward filial disobedience.
                              —*Northanger Abbey*

Dear Jane Austen,

I am twenty-one years old and madly in love. My
boyfriend is a great guy who is planning a career in
the military. He currently attends one of the military
academies. The problem is my family. They do not
want me to marry him because of his career. They say
he will never make any money and that I am not cut
out to be a military wife (I am headed to Wharton next
year for an MBA.) I know my parents only want the
best for me and it kills me to go against their wishes
but I think I am old enough to know what is right for
me. Kevin has asked me to marry him. My heart says
yes—should I follow it even if it means completely
alienating my family?

Navy Blue

~~&~~

Dear Blue Heroine,

First of all, allow me to commend you on your taste in suitors.

Two of my own dear brothers—Frank and Charles—are naval men and I do not believe the world holds a higher calling for a man than that profession. It is true that my girls marry gentlemen from other fields of endeavour—clergymen and country landowners—but have you ever heard me admire more fervently any hero's occupation than I do that of the sailors in *The Elliots*—that is, *Persuasion*? Captain Frederick Wentworth and his fellow sailors unite some of the finest qualities to be found in their sex. Why, even Henry Crawford, rich and free of all worldly obligations, envies the hard, dangerous life of Fanny's sailor brother:

The glory of heroism, of usefulness, of exertion, of endurance, made his own habits of selfish indulgence appear in shameful contrast; and he wished he had been a William Price, distinguishing himself and working his way to fortune and consequence with so much self-respect and happy ardour, instead of what he was!

Although Crawford's yearning after heroism lasts but a moment before he lapses back into contentment with wealth, privilege, and unheroic ease, his admiration of William is an impulse from the nobler part of the man, a part that should have been attended to more often. If your young man belongs to that higher breed that chooses a life of honor, courage, and heroic endeavour over one of mere money-making and luxury, then he is a man indeed, and you have chosen well if he also returns your affection. Your parents' fears are understandable but not therefore to rule your life.

If you will permit me, Blue Heroine, I shall expand the second part of my answer to cover the wider question of filial disobedience for the sake of all my heroines-in-training who have written to me about this matter in all its various forms. In my novels,

written in a world where women's choices were almost all to do with marriage, the question manifests
itself almost exclusively in matrimonial affairs.

Must a young heroine acquiesce to the wishes of
her guardians even when she believes them to be
wrong? Is it likely that a young girl would know better, make wiser choices, than those who have lived in
the world for twice as long, and more? I refer you to
my novels, where my opinion could not be more
plainly expressed. But let me begin by saying that
you are full young (for your era though not for mine)
to be getting married. Still, girls of fifteen or sixteen
who disobey their guardians in pursuit of a passion
(Georgiana Darcy, Lydia Bennet, Colonel Brandon's
Eliza) are not merely young but foolish also; they are
not proved wrong simply because they are young. In
such cases this wilful disobedience is wrong when
viewed from any angle and can in no way be justified.
Marianne Dashwood, though not quite so young,
displays a similar wilfulness in her pursuit of Willoughby. For some girls, rebellion against authority—
parental or societal—is often an intrinsic part of the
romance in such situations and you must ask yourself if you are not saying, along with Lindsay from
Love and Freindship (a work not entirely without wit
though I was a mere child myself when I wrote it): "No
never...Lady Dorothea is lovely and Engaging; I prefer
no woman to her; but know Sir, that I scorn to marry
her in compliance with your wishes. No! Never shall it
be said that I obliged my Father." With the same
perverse impulse, some girls will like a man more the
more that is urged against him by their elders.

Marianne excepted, my *heroines* are not guided by
mere wilfulness in making such decisions. As Elizabeth Bennet's Aunt Gardiner says to her: "You are too
sensible a girl, Lizzy, to fall in love merely because
you are warned against it..." And when Elizabeth
disobeys her mother's command that she accept a
proposal of marriage from the preposterous Mr.
Collins, no one *but* her mother could accuse her of
doing the wrong thing. To be sure, that situation is

rather a joke, as Mr. Bennet's response to it shows. Every reader will remember the lines... Well, just in case, do allow me to indulge my vanity by quoting them here, like a mother repeating to all who will listen the clever prattle of a favourite child:

"An unhappy alternative is before you, Elizabeth. From this day you must be a stranger to one of your parents.—Your mother will never see you again if you do *not* marry Mr. Collins, and I will never see you again if you *do*."

Ah, I confess, those lines never fail to amuse me. There are, however, two more serious attempts to influence my heroines to act against their own wishes in the question of matrimony. One is a matter of persuasion in favor of a suitor, the other against.

Sir Thomas Bertram, more beloved by Fanny than her natural father, attacks her in a very vulnerable spot when he urges her to accept Henry Crawford's proposal against her inclination:

Her heart was almost broke by such a picture of what she appeared to him; by such accusations, so heavy, so multiplied, so rising in dreadful gradation! Self-willed, obstinate, selfish, and ungrateful. He thought her all this.

Yet my Fanny, though it breaks her heart to disappoint her beloved uncle so bitterly, knows that it is wrong to marry without affection, and even these, the strongest incentives imaginable to her tender nature, cannot persuade her to go against her conscience. She refuses to do as her guardian wishes, requests, and quite nearly demands, and she is right in her refusal. Every reader, no matter how strong their dislike of my heroine, must feel it to be so. (Frank Churchill's cowardly failure to disobey his adoptive parents when they ask him to go against *his* conscience shows that he has not the character to be worthy of Emma. Yet how many of you believe Frank, because he possesses the playful wit that Fanny lacks, to be the superior being? Ah, that is my own doing, I concede. In imagining otherwise I look about with diligence and success for great evil where it is not in reality to be found. As such judgments are made in the world, so I take care to lay the foundation for them in my novels.)

And now to the other side of the matter, the one that more closely reflects your own dilemma: is parental disapproval of a suitor whom a heroine loves sufficient cause for her to refuse his offer of marriage? Are guardians always the best judges in such matters? As it happens, I have just finished writing a novel about this very theme. Let me read to you from the end: "Bad Morality again. A young Woman proved to have had more discrimination of Character than her elder—to have seen in two Instances more clearly what it was about than her Godmother!" In one instance Anne Elliot sees the good in a man, in the other the evil, where her Godmother, though wise and good in other matters, is blind... But wait...before I continue...that sounds a bit too explicit, does it not? My readers do not need such directing posts. I believe I shall cancel this passage. Indeed, I begin to think I shall revise the ending entirely. I do not like the way my hero and heroine come to an understanding at last. I wrote "Finis" but this morning while Fanny sat just there and now I believe I must return to this manuscript. I am tired, though. How these aches and pains trouble my thoughts and slow my pen. I begin to fear I shall be like my dear mother, nearing eight decades and imagining illness and indisposition when I am in truth as healthy as a Highbury ox.

There, the passage is gone. But still it contains my views—all too clearly. Although a perfect world would hold none but perfect parents, in reality children are often wiser than their guardians, and I cannot support a general rule that would declare the necessity of unfailing filial obedience. Although Anne never complains about her decision to accept Lady Russell's guidance, she knows she would never give such overly prudent advice to someone in a similar situation herself: "...how eloquent...were her wishes on the side of early warm attachment, and a cheerful confidence in futurity, against that over-anxious caution which seems to insult exertion and distrust Providence!" Early warm attachment...how much unhappiness is purchased with its sacrifice! If a young man I once knew—a man, mind you, and not even a young woman, from whom obedience would more naturally be expected—if this young man had had the courage to stand up to his uncle and say that he *should* have the girl he loved and damn those who would keep him from her...why, even mild-mannered Henry Tilney opposed his father's unreasonable objection to his choice of a bride. Ah, Tom, would that you had been more heroic and less prudent when we were young! My life would have been very different. But then the world would never have known Anne Elliot. An unhappy alternative indeed. But our mutual indifference was established decades ago, enough time, I imagine, to change every pore of one's skin and every feeling of one's mind. Pray, forgive me for mentioning him now... To marry without love is wrong but to be kept from marrying by over-cautiousness, prudence, and a lack of faith—that is a road to the deepest regret.

My heroines love their parents and obey them— even when there is some difference of opinion—in almost all circumstances. But my novels show that mothers and fathers and guardians can be and often are foolish themselves. Think of Mrs. Allen, Mr. and Mrs. Bennet, Mrs. Dashwood, and Mr. Woodhouse, to name but a few. Some of my heroines, like Fanny Price and Anne Elliot, are so unlucky as to receive poor guidance from both natural parents AND surrogate guardians. Try very hard not to be ignorant and foolish yourself, my Blue Heroine. To you and to all my heroines-in-training, I say: read my novels, learn about the world, and cultivate your own judgment.

Yours very sincerely,

Jane Austen

> **JANE AUSTEN SAYS: WHEN A HEROINE IS SATISFIED THAT SHE HAS EXERCISED JUDGMENT WITH CLEAR VISION, MORAL PRINCIPLE, AND COMMON SENSE, SHE NEED NOT ACQUIESCE TO OPPOSING VIEWPOINTS.**

Dear Jane Austen,

Is it wrong for me to date my sister's ex-boyfriend? She says she doesn't want me to because he is a jerk (in your language a cad, a reprobate) and she is only concerned for my welfare but I think she's just jealous and I want to keep dating him. Is there some rule to follow here?

Sister Troubles in New York City

~~&~~

Dear Troubled Heroine,

If you lived in a remote, sparsely populated region of America I would see your predicament in a more understanding light. Country villages, such as those in which I have largely spent my days, generally contain few enough marriageable gentlemen, and it may well be that one sister has little choice but to pick a suitor who has at one time exhibited a real or fancied attachment to another. But in your country's largest city? I find it rather difficult to believe that there is not some dubious motive at work on your part, and I beg you to ask yourself if you have not a desire to create some family discord. (It is beyond my comprehension how you all cram onto that small island. It is quite as bad as London for noise and dirt. With no birds or flowers or quiet garden I should soon hang myself—in which plan I would no doubt be thwarted by the want of a tree within miles.) But if you can acquit yourself of any malicious motive, or, indeed, of an innocent because unrecognized need to claim what once belonged to your sister, then I shall answer at greater length.

There is no rule, necessarily, whereby one sister is forbidden to look upon a man once attached to another as a potential suitor. No rule, that is, that serves for all cases. But observe the outcome of such situations as they arise in my novels and you will see that for one reason or another, things simply do not turn out very well.

Lydia Bennet, coarse, wild, selfish, and ignorant, succeeds in snaring Colonel Wickham, a man with whom her sister Elizabeth was briefly infatuated. Wickham's feelings for Lydia sank into indifference soon after their marriage. And how could they not, with the example of the vastly superior sister, with whom he had previously been on such friendly terms, in his memory and sometimes before his eyes? ...By the bye, I have actually heard it bruited about that my darling Elizabeth was *jealous* because Lydia succeeded with Wickham where she could not. To be sure, Elizabeth is a little drier even than usual when speaking of her youngest sister's marriage, but as to jealousy, I hardly think it in keeping with a heroine's dignity...well, we need not settle the question. Other examples will do for us nicely. Upon my word, I believe there are one or two occasions where my characters are truer to life than quite suits me. George Henry Lewes said I was the most *real* of all writers, and he was married (after a fashion, that is) to George Eliot. (I grant again that she is a fine authoress, but does it not strike you that there is too much moral instruction in her novels? They would suit Fanny Price perfectly but I confess my own taste is for somewhat lighter and livelier fare that is nonetheless perfectly real.)

Mansfield Park's Julia Bertram is certainly jealous of her sister Maria once Henry Crawford makes clear his preference for the latter: "Her heart was sore and angry... The sister with whom she was used to be on easy terms, was now become her greatest enemy..." Julia longs for Maria's punishment while for her part

"Maria felt her triumph, and pursued her purpose careless of Julia..." Perhaps, Troubled Heroine, you and your sister have more affection, and more principle, than to stoop to such mean feelings. But your letter—forgive me for saying what will be unwelcome—betrays at least the possibility that such is not the case.

Anne Elliot was Charles Musgrove's first choice for a wife and their relationship remains cordial though she refused him and he subsequently married her sister Mary. But the marriage is troubled. Husband and wife torment each other a good deal of the time. Now, Mary's nature is not the best to begin with but even a more generous spirit would find it hard to tolerate with good humour the continual reminder in the person of her sister that she was not her husband's first choice. Moreover, Charles's sisters Louisa and Henrietta make no effort to conceal their decided preference for Anne, wishing aloud that she had accepted their brother's proposal. All parties involved are good people, and yet the situation invites discord. Penelope Watson is much more malicious: she deliberately schemes to destroy her sister's prospects in hopes of winning the gentleman in question as her own suitor. She succeeds only in the first part of her plan, and Elizabeth Watson thereafter holds that her sister has ruined her happiness, for which she cannot forgive her. When their sister Emma hears of all this, she is quite shocked: "Could a sister do such a thing?—Rivalry, treachery between sisters!" And that, my dear, is the proper response for a heroine to have.

Your sister objects to this relationship. Are you quite sure the reason she gives has no merit? A man who lives amongst such a great number of eligible young ladies who would address his attentions to one sister soon after ending his involvement with another is at the very least guilty of a certain indelicacy of feeling. It has an odd look—are you quite sure of the innocence of his motives? There is implication enough to go around in this matter. Do not flatter yourself with the fancy that between you and this man is a

pure passion, unadulterated by anything external to
it—such as his prior relationship with your sister. If
she is unhappy about it, do give her the benefit of the
doubt and at least entertain the possibility that her
reasons have validity. If the prospect of distressing
your sister, perhaps ruining her happiness forever,
does not put a blight on your romantic vision; if this
gentleman's character truly bears up under honest
scrutiny; if you are persuaded that you could not be
happy without him, and, further, that your own
motives are pure, then you may proceed... I hear
visitors approaching.

Come in. My dear niece Anna! How lovely to see you. And
you have brought your father with you. Come in, please.
From the damp, windblown look of you we are still being
treated to November in July. Yes, my love, you may read it. I
would not expose my modest efforts to every one, but I
know what a lively interest you have in my writing. I do not
suppose you ever have a chance to write stories yourself
now you are a wife and mother. You are a fine writer, just
like you, James. Indeed you are, my brother, and that you
are perfectly aware of the fact I can read in your eyes. Do
you honestly want her to read it aloud? Very well. I bow to
my eldest brother's commands... Ah, I had forgotten. Anna,
I am sorry to interrupt, but would you be so kind as to fetch
my shawl from the drawing room? ...Dearest James, while
she is gone allow me to beg your pardon. The subject
touches home. But after all these years I little thought...you
too were enchanted by Eliza, were not you? What a
creature, to receive proposals from two such fine young
men—and brothers! But she would not have suited you, or
Steventon, you know. Well, perhaps you are right there—
Steventon would not have suited her. I am sorry. I did not
know the wound had been so deep. You always were
sensitive. How we writers pay for our retentive feelings!
   Here is Anna back again. Thank you, my dear. My
mother says I must go downstairs at once? No doubt she
commands me on the grounds that I have always written in
the sitting-room, and while she undoubtedly admits to a
prodigious amount of company in the house today, she
nonetheless says I have never been a fine lady of sensibility

and that I shall not begin putting on such airs now. Now, were those not her words? Anna, you did not tell her I was not well! That will never do. Your grandmamma will be leaving the only sofa for me and you know I do very well reclining on my three chairs. You may tell her that I do indeed write up here when I have a particular need for quiet, and there is a monstrous deal of noise downstairs today. Even she could not imagine a creaking door sufficient warning for me to hide my writing from such a crowd. Must I announce my arrangements to the world? I assure you I am not at all ill.

Now, your father has persuaded me that I should add a few lines to this reply, though you may be sure it cost him a blush to discuss such matters. I shall read them to you as I write:

> But, Troubled Heroine, is it worth it? You may have no idea of the wound you would inflict—are even now inflicting—upon your sister. Are there no other men, of all the millions in your city alone (where people from all walks of life mingle in a manner unthinkable in my day) who would answer? Although there is no absolute moral injunction against this attachment, I foresee trouble if you proceed with it, and advise you to break off the connection now.

> I remain yours very sincerely,

> Jane Austen

JANE AUSTEN SAYS: A HEROINE IS NOT HER SISTER'S RIVAL IN LOVE.

Is that improved, James? Anna, you smile. Did not you know your father was such a fine counselor to lovers? This visit has been delightful but, Anna, you well know that my mother loves you best of all her grandchildren so you had better go back downstairs and entertain her again. I am very glad to learn of the rice pudding and Stilton cheese—no bad life here at Chawton Cottage! Come back a bit later and I shall read to you some more, and find out how you like being a married lady. James, you return to Steventon directly? My best love to my sister Mary and little Caroline. Make everyone at Steventon admire *Emma* beyond any thing. Anna, do assure my mother I am quite well!

They have gone. Poor animal. She is already becoming quite worn out with children. To be sure, I am glad to have so many fine brothers and a peerless sister, but having witnessed so many women die bringing their children into the world, I know very well the cost of a large family. I never much wanted to lay in myself. At least I have escaped *that*.

Dear Jane Austen,

I come from the world's most dysfunctional family. My father gambles and cheats on my mother, who curses at him and beats him when she drinks. My brothers become physically and verbally abusive to each other and to their sisters with little provocation. But I have little sympathy for my sisters because they are so cruel and selfish. My fiancé's family is just the opposite: very loving, stable, and supportive. I am ready to make a long-awaited escape from the past and embark on a glorious new life completely sepa-rate from our families. Who needs them? But my fiancé not only wants his family involved in our lives—he thinks I should try to stay close to my fam-ily too. He says family is family, no matter what. Tell me, Miss Austen, must blood ties supersede all other claims? Can I cut myself off from my horrific family and still have a heroine's happy ending?

Orphan Wannabe

Dear Orphan Heroine,

A heroine will always have some measure of love for her family and take an interest in their welfare, even when they are derelict in fulfilling their own familial obligations. But she also has the sense to judge people on their own merits without regard to blood connection. If position within a family alone would determine the amount of love and esteem given someone, parents would not have favourite children—as they certainly do—but would look upon all their offspring with equal affection. (In my own family my mother preferred James. You see, my mother is quite a good writer herself—she has written some firstrate verses indeed—and James showed great promise in that line. More than promise—to be just, he was accomplished in his own way. One would perhaps think that she might have found equal satisfaction in the scribblings of another of her children and shown him—or her—some special favor too... My father's favourite was Henry, and with good cause. Not merely for his charm is he my favorite also. No, he has done more to see that the world is acquainted with my darling children than any living being. You may wonder if I have a favourite amongst *them*. I should not like to say...though, perhaps...no, I shall *not* say.)

Sometimes indeed the preference for one family member over another shows devotion far in excess of what is truly deserved, and thus appears quite inexplicable. (The blameless brother of the Prodigal Son can give you a full accounting of this puzzling if not infuriating occurrence.) Amongst my heroines, Emma dotes on her father excessively. My readers have said that it is simply not normal for a lively, clever girl of twenty-one to weep over the very thought of quitting her father to marry a man she loves—a man, moreover, who returns her affection. Indeed, Emma determines quite seriously never to do so. But does not such an irrational excess of filial devotion only add to dear Emma's appeal? And yet, Mr. Woodhouse has not been a very good father. With his weak intellect, depressed spirits, valetudinarian ways, and selfish insistence upon everyone's acquiescence to what in fact suits only him, he joins the ranks of the many other bad parents and guardians in my novels.

Upon my word, I do not know why my books are so full of bad parents. My own mother and dear departed father cannot be touched for decency, industry, piety, wit, and affection and yet I rarely give such qualities to my maternal and paternal characters. Consider the women: Mrs. Allen is no proper guardian at all for young Catherine Morland, and even Catherine's own mother, though a very good sort of woman in her way, has not the wit to see her daughter's heart though it is prominently displayed on her sleeve! Mrs. Bennet is a silly, vain, vulgar woman and her mismanagement of her daughters' upbringing almost ruins the family. Her husband's indolence is equally inexcusable. And as for Lady Susan, well, she is downright wicked in her treatment of her daughter—yes, quite delightfully wicked... I beg your pardon. I did not mean to praise her monstrous behaviour in any way. She was the creation of a flurry of youthful rebelliousness against morality and propriety. A juvenile work to be sure—but it does amuse me to see how very much thoroughly scandalous behaviour interested me then. I do not mean to digress once again: I need not go through all my novels: a moment's consideration will show you that each of my heroines suffers to a greater or lesser degree from lapses in parental responsibility. And so it is in the world outside my novels.

Heroines love their parents regardless of such shortcomings. But while they love and accept the person without condition, they are not entirely blind to their failings and seek to correct them, particularly when doing so will serve a greater good. Thus, Elizabeth Bennet tries correctly though unsuccessfully to persuade her father that Lydia's trip to Brighton is not to be contemplated, and that it is his bounden duty to exert his parental authority over her in the matter.

Where feasible, heroines similarly aim to improve the manners, morals, and situations of their siblings, whom they also love despite their often serious flaws—as Elizabeth tries with varying degrees of success to improve her younger sisters. Elinor Dashwood strenuously attempts to teach her sister Marianne to exercise a reasonable degree of restraint in her dangerous intimacy with Willoughby. Anne Elliot continuously works to improve the behaviour of her sisters, and Fanny Price is quite preoccupied with the welfare of her brother William and sister Susan. But sometimes characters are simply impervious to good influence. If I thought you would meet with success I would urge you not to abandon your family to degradation and ruin but I dare say in your case the attempt would be futile. So, continue to love them and be of service to them where it will truly do them good, but do not feel—if you will forgive a naval analogy—that you must go down with the ship. Save yourself. Stay away from your family if that is what is required, once having assured yourself that you have done all you can to contribute to their physical, moral, and emotional welfare.

We Austens have never been sentimental about such matters. I am quite appalled when I see how my novels have been softened and sweetened, particularly in your era's dramatic productions—although I must say, that was a lovely rendering of *The Elliots*— that is, *Persuasion*—in the last decade of the twentieth century. And as acting seldom satisfies me, that is high praise indeed. To be sure, the image of my heroine kissing her hero on a Bath street rather surprised me, but I am not such a prude as to think it so very bad. Kissing where there is true affection is the most exhilarating experience I know of, surpassing even dancing, I think, for excitement. I have not always been an old maid, you know—that idea is not unlike the legend of your first president's perfect veracity.

It is not only parents who fail to act as good family members: my novels are also full of brothers and sisters who behave perhaps not quite so badly as yours, dear Orphan Wannabe, but very far from any model for sibling behaviour. The brother and sister of Catherine Morland's friend Isabella Thorpe behave towards each other with a shocking lack of consideration. Within Elizabeth Bennet's own family, the sisters exhibit behaviour towards each other that ranges from very bad to very good: Lydia is so inconsiderate as to say and do things she knows will cause her sisters pain. Elizabeth, on the other hand, turns down Mr. Darcy's first proposal primarily on the grounds that he has ruined her dear sister Jane's chance for happiness with Mr. Bingley by persuading the man she loves to forget about her.

As I mentioned in response to Troubled Heroine, Julia and Maria Bertram are very bad sisters. In addition to their rivalry over Henry Crawford, they respond perversely to their brother Tom's serious illness, preferring to stay away enjoying themselves in London rather than attend at his bedside. Indeed, they have had no good models for sisterhood in their mother and aunts. To Lady Bertram and Mrs. Norris, where their sister Mrs. Price and her family were concerned, "...the ties of blood were little more than nothing." They are not alone in my novels in feeling so. Given the rivalry and treachery amongst sisters in the Watson household, it is with good reason Emma Watson feels "that a family party might be the worst of all parties." I understand that in the twentieth century Anne Elliot was often referred to by critics as a kind of Cinderella: Mary and particularly Elizabeth would indeed serve as model wicked stepsisters, though they are in fact related to my heroine by blood.

And do not think only sisters behave badly: in addition to John Thorpe, who mocks his sisters as well as his mother, John Dashwood serves his sisters Elinor and Marianne very badly indeed when he allows his wife to talk him out of giving them the annuity that he knows full well is his moral obligation.

But there is good news here: blood ties do not necessarily determine the degree of affection, admiration, and well-earned gratitude my heroines will have for an individual. Elizabeth Bennet's aunt and uncle are far better guardians and companions than her mother and father. These are of course close relations, but not the closest. Sir Thomas and Lady Bertram, though by no means perfect, are nonetheless better parents to Fanny than her natural parents. She in turn is a better daughter than Maria and Julia Bertram. Lady Russell loves Anne Elliot more than her father does and Anne prefers the entire amiable, loving Musgrove family to her own, judging Mr. and Mrs. Musgrove to be better parents than her father: "They do every thing to confer happiness..." she says of them warmly; "What a blessing to young people to be in such hands!" (Indeed, I fear I was rather hard on good Mrs. Musgrove. Although she certainly deluded herself about the worth of her loutish sailor son, perhaps a mother, at least, ought to be allowed prejudice where her children are concerned. It is a difficult matter to decide.)

Blood ties are not always the strongest ones, and dearer relationships are even more common in the world than in my novels. You may find in your husband's good family the affection and respect you miss in your own....

Now here is Cass again, come to scold her sister for neglecting our company. I shall ask her if that is not true....

Ah, no. I beg your pardon. She has come on a charitable mission, to see if my little aches are still troubling me, and to soothe me into tolerable comfort. I have thanked her and assured her I feel very well. There is no need for her to physic me. Writing to my heroines-in-training refreshes me as much as a month at Bath refreshes a gouty old baronet. So, off she goes again to attend to another troublesome relation.

Ah, my Orphan Heroine, if you only knew the blessed joy of having a loving sister—particularly an elder sister who dotes on you and allows you to tease her with endless saucy remarks. To be sure, the sweetest companionship in my novels is between sisters. Elizabeth and Jane Bennet are model sisters for any heroine. And what man in *Sense and Sensibility* ever displays the affection Elinor has for her younger sister, shown most powerfully when she watches over Marianne as the poor girl lies ill and wretched and fearfully close to death? Brother and sister share an almost equally close bond. Fanny Price loves Edmund Bertram because he was like a brother to her as they grew up. Yet he is not her brother and he causes her grief. Her love for this brother-like figure does not equal the passion she shows for her real brother, William. No romantic love in that novel touches their level of mutual devotion and interest: "Children of the same family, the same blood, with the same first associations and habits, have some means of enjoyment in their power, which no subsequent connections can supply..."

And how should I not betray that these fraternal relationships, sister and sister, brother and sister, are the most precious to me? I shall tell you something Cass said. Charles, my sweet baby brother, reported it back to me: she said I was "...the sun of [her] life, the gilder of every pleasure, the soother of every sorrow..." What lover ever heard higher praise? Blessed with such a family, I can only hope not to survive them or their affection.

Do not abandon your family, dear Orphan Wannabe, while there is the smallest hope you can reclaim even the least amount of such precious love for them and for yourself.

Yours affectionately,

Jane Austen

**JANE AUSTEN SAYS: A HEROINE DOES NOT
ABANDON HER FAMILY.**

Chapter Three
A Heroine and Her Friends

It had been a friend and companion such as few possessed, intelligent, well-informed, useful, gentle, knowing all the ways of the family, interested in all its concerns, and peculiarly interested in herself, in every pleasure, ever scheme of her's; —one to whom she could speak every thought as it arose, and who had such an affection for her as could never find fault.

—Emma

Dear Jane Austen,

I have a girlfriend who really bugs me. She doesn't return my phone calls, drops me when more fashionable friends come along, and flirts with boys I like. But other times she's so sweet and so much fun to be with. That's when she calls me her best friend. Sometimes I think she's using me when she has no one else and I should cut her off but I don't really have many other friends and I need someone to go out with.

What do you think, Miss Austen? Is a fair weather friend better than none?

A Friend in Need

~~&~~

Dear Friendly Heroine,

I must say, the description of your "friend" has a familiar ring. Is not her model Isabella Thorpe, young Catherine Morland's "dear, dear" friend in *Northanger Abbey*? So long as Catherine is useful to Isabella, the latter is happy to link arms with her and parade through the streets and assembly rooms of Bath sharing whispers about horrid Gothic novels and handsome young men. But Isabella, as all my readers know, is a false friend, scheming and affected in all her ways. Moreover, she invariably serves Catherine badly, giving her, after Henry Tilney has left Bath with no mention of a return, "every possible encouragement to continue to think of him." Thus, "...his impression on her fancy was not suffered to weaken." This is not the behaviour of a true friend, who would rather urge Catherine not to think of the young man until she had confirmation that she was on his mind as well.

Catherine is merely seventeen, diffident and naïve, so the handsome and lively Miss Thorpe is able to impose upon her for rather longer than any of my other heroines would allow. Catherine is seduced by the beautiful older girl's charm and superficial sweetness. But even Catherine recognizes the superiority of a true friend like Eleanor Tilney, and eventually breaks with Isabella, having learned a hard lesson: that while an open, trusting nature is a good thing to have, a heroine must not allow herself to be used by others. Once a heroine has been mistreated, and if she is assured that the cause of her distress is not a simple misunderstanding, she does not tarry to be abused again. A heroine, my dear, has self-respect, and you are not behaving like one if you meekly accept your so-called friend's mistreatment. And if you maintain this friendship simply because you have no other companions, you have no reason to complain of her doing the same by you. In short, you must put an end to this intimacy now.

Catherine is certainly not alone amongst my heroines in finding it necessary to end a friendship.

Emma must let her intimacy with Harriet Smith quietly sink. I am sorry to say that in that case it was my peerless girl herself who was—though, I hasten to add, with only the very best of intentions—the false friend. Right, as usual, was Mr. Knightley when he told her with characteristic bluntness, "You have been no friend to Harriet Smith." The fears he confided to Mrs. Weston about Harriet proved well founded: "I think her the very worst sort of companion that Emma could possibly have." It sometimes happens that friendships must end in this way, without the assignment of blame, simply because one or both of the parties involved no longer finds satisfaction in the connection. No friendship stands still: a heroine can expect her friendships to alter over time in more or less dramatic ways.

Another and a far more complicated example of a vexed friendship is that between Elizabeth Bennet and Charlotte Lucas. You will recall that the two girls are very close friends at the beginning of *Pride and Prejudice*, speaking to one another with affection, good humour, and unreserve. Elizabeth is shocked and disgusted when she discovers that Charlotte has agreed to marry the odious Mr. Collins:

She had always felt that Charlotte's opinion of matrimony was not exactly like her own, but she could not have supposed it possible that when called into action, she would have sacrificed every better feeling to worldly advantage.

Dear Elizabeth, she is blinded by prejudice in this, as in other instances, you know, for Charlotte's behaviour here is "inconsistent" and "unaccountable" as she later calls it, only insofar as Lizzy habitually dismisses the evidence of her own eyes and ears when it contradicts her established beliefs: "You know…that you would never act in this way yourself," she told Charlotte after Charlotte expressed an opinion about marriage contrary to Elizabeth's own. The event proved Elizabeth to be in error, of course, and by no means for the last time.

As a result of this engagement, Charlotte is "sunk in her esteem" and "...Elizabeth felt persuaded that no real confidence could ever subsist between them again." While this may seem harsh, Friendly Heroine, and Elizabeth's warm feelings for Charlotte do revive to some degree, it is true that the friendship is never the same. This might be a difficult matter for people of your era to understand, but if you wish to be a heroine you must make the attempt: although Charlotte continues to behave towards Elizabeth in the same manner as before her engagement, her actions reveal a character that is not the superior one Elizabeth thought it to be. A heroine chooses her friends not merely on the basis of their behaviour towards herself, but on how they behave in general. A woman may behave particularly well towards you and yet be quite a bad person. No doubt the world's greatest villains behaved well towards some chosen favourites. Just as you would not overlook moral failings in a suitor simply because he showed a flattering preference for you, so you must judge a friend with a similar degree of detachment. Do not discriminate so little as to allow everyone who desires your friendship to secure it. General benevolence, but not general friendship, make a heroine what she ought to be.

But no one is without fault. (I ask you again: did any novelist before me ever acknowledge as I do the mixed characters of all real people?) Thus, Mrs. Weston's too-indulgent treatment of Emma, and Lady Russell's snobbery, which taints her advice to Anne, are, weighed in the balance, not so serious as to be grounds for ending friendships so full of mutual affection and esteem. But, even putting aside the question of their rivalry in love, Mary Crawford, for all her superficial charm and even her real kindness towards Fanny, is shown by her cold, heartless, calculating, mercenary behaviour at other times to be unworthy of our heroine's friendship. So... What is this paper lying at my feet? At first I thought it must be another letter from a heroine-in-training but indeed it is not: it is a precious letter from my own dear friend Anne, that is, Miss Sharp. Anne Sharp was our

Fanny's governess for a time, you know. I met her at my brother Edward's house, magnificent Godmersham. A clever, hardworking woman with no family of her own. With few exceptions, my dearest friends have been members of my own family—Cass and Fanny and Anna and Henry and poor dear Eliza, cousin, sister, and friend united. But Miss Sharp—now that is another kind of friendship altogether. I understand that in your era, Friendly Heroine, many women remain single or, divorce being rather more common than it is now in 1816, lose their husbands without the necessity of wearing black crape. I therefore advise you to cultivate worthy friends who will answer on those occasions—and indeed, there may be many—when you are without a husband or lover, when you will have, perhaps, no children of your own to amuse and engross you, when sister and brother, dear though they be, will not answer your particular need for companionship. Then, the incomparable worth of a sensible, resourceful woman like Anne Sharp, always the comforter of those near to her in their distresses, will be clear to you.

Women in your era are abroad in the great world with more opportunity to make acquaintance outside of their immediate circle of family and neighbors. And you are luckier than I in this respect too: your society places more value on working women, and on single, childless women, than does my own. For when Emma Watson boldly declares that she would rather teach than marry a man she does not like, her more experienced older sister wisely replies: "I would rather do anything than be a teacher at a school." Two hundred years before your time, marriage and teaching were almost the only choices for women of education and no independent means of living, and teachers led a terrible life indeed. And yet, though I longed for Anne's employer to fall in love with her and remove her from the dreary life of a working spinster, Emma Watson's instincts are right, you know. Clever women need not be ashamed of the depth of their resources or their desire to marshall them in the cause of happiness. My own widowed great-grandmother, as I told one of your sister heroines-in-training, ran a school quite creditably. Mrs. Weston, Emma's beloved friend whom I just mentioned, was of course a governess, as indeed the beautiful and talented Jane Fairfax is destined to be. The position itself can be pitiful, to be sure—Jane Fairfax compares it to the slave trade—but those called to it are often quite superior—as in the case of Anne Sharp. But I beg your pardon: again I stray from the subject at hand.

You do not say, Freindly (Forgive me. Spelling was not my best subject. But you know, we were not so particular about it as you are. And if, at times, I choose to adopt the orthographic customs of my American correspondents, do not beat me.) ...You do not say, Friendly Heroine, whether or not you are single. But married, single, or something in between, you are quite right to consider your friendships with other women as holding nearly the same degree of importance as your romantic attachments. For you will discover, if you have not already, that throughout your life you will have need of friends no matter how fond you and your hero—should you attach one—are of each other. For heroes will almost always be occupied in the world more than heroines, more focused on success and achievement in affairs unconnected with their nearest and dearest at home. Politics, war, business, finance, property, sport—as I well know from my brothers—all will distract your hero from you, and at such times you must allow him to be distracted. Rather than let feelings of abandonment prey upon you during those periods when gentlemen are off hunting foxes, and fighting wars, and making speeches, and lending money, you must rather turn to diversions of your own. Being women, we are not so fond of solitary diversions. Heroines love to visit warehouses in search of sprigged muslins and satin ribbons; to dance with handsome young men even when they are not in love with them; to take tea with other heroines and gossip; to walk in the garden amidst the primroses and hyacinths, arm in arm with a friend, and gossip; to attend the theatre and between acts search the boxes across the way for subjects of—yes, though I blush to confess it since it is injurious to a heroine's dignity—gossip. Excursions to scenes of beauty—to the Lakes or, more glorious still, to the sea—all these activities must fill those hours when your hero is engrossed by his battles in the great world. There are some women, more in your day than in mine, who have such battles to fight themselves. (Indeed, my own life has not been so confined to the domestic sphere as many believe.) But even these dragon-slaying heroines are women still, and they will need good friends like Eleanor Tilney—like Anne Sharp.

Your faithful friend,

Jane Austen

> **JANE AUSTEN SAYS: A HEROINE NEEDS GOOD FRIENDS AS MUCH AS SHE NEEDS A HERO.**

I hear footsteps on the stairs. Surely that is Martha going down the hall to her bedroom. How appropriate that Martha Lloyd should pass my door at this moment, my friend and sister under every circumstance, and the model in truth for the best friend a heroine could have. None of my heroines have friends of such sterling character as Martha. She and Cass both help Cook with the meals, you know, and leave me, very kindly, to my writing. I do not deserve such particular treatment, but I am not fool enough to refuse it. Martha has been my good friend for almost my entire life. I took to her from the first, though she is ten years older than I. Her sister—that is, James's Mary—was the likelier choice for a friend but somehow...but never mind. She is not on the whole a liberal-minded woman, but she is my sister now and I shall say nothing unkind of her. As to Martha, ten years are nothing, you know, when souls are *sympathique*, as Eliza, another dear, dear friend of mine, would say. Little did Martha and I imagine (I was but twenty-three) when we snuggled in bed laughing and talking until two o'clock, that we should be living together in this way, sharing our lives with each other and no man. Ah, well... Many of my correspondents today—those who chase men, or who torture them—will find the arrangement offers a comfortable alternative to married life.

Dear Jane Austen,

How honest should friends be with one another? I have been criticized for being uncommunicative with my friends, for hiding my feelings, but I'm just being myself, a quiet, private person. Is that so bad?

Reserved

~~&~~

Dear Reserved Heroine,

You are reserved indeed, for you have kept from me any details that would enlighten me with respect to the situation about which you enquire. I shall therefore take into account in my answer a great variety of possibilities. Let us take the example of Elizabeth Bennet just set forth. Although, in general, Elizabeth—as Lady Catherine says—gives her opinion very decidedly for so young a person, she can nonetheless keep her thoughts to herself when she believes reserve to be the best course. So while the news of Charlotte Lucas's engagement to Mr. Collins is an unpleasant shock, for Charlotte's sake, Elizabeth, after that first moment of unguarded incredulity, gives voice to her disapproval only in the company of her discreet sister Jane. Were Elizabeth to express her disapprobation openly, it would not dissuade Charlotte from the union but only cause her pain. Where disapprobation is certain to do no good, but on the contrary merely cause unhappiness, complete openness is usually not desirable.

Elinor Dashwood is accused by her sister Marianne of an ungenerous reserve, of having "confidence in no one," but Elinor's reserve is not merely a natural inclination to secrecy but in fact the result of a great effort. She knows that her unhappiness, if revealed, would hurt her sister and mother, and therefore she keeps it hidden. Marianne, on the contrary concealing nothing, thinks not at all of the anguish her open expression of grief is causing her family. Aware that she is "giving pain every moment to her mother and sisters," she nonetheless wilfully courts misery and in their presence seeks increase of wretchedness. I believe it is quite obvious which I hold to be the better course for a heroine.

Because she knows Lady Russell had only her dear Anne's best interest at heart when she offered the advice, Anne Elliot does not reproach her friend for ruining her best chance for happiness in persuading her not to marry Frederick Wentworth. To broach the subject would only serve to cause the older woman pain and could do no possible good. So the two never speak of the matter. Indeed, "the subject was never alluded to."

Emma Woodhouse dislikes Jane Fairfax, who (rather than Harriet Smith) should have been her first choice for a friend, because she is cold, cautious, "disgustingly" reserved. Emma herself suppresses her real opinion on many occasions, even with her very good friend Mrs. Weston, but there is a difference: she does so out of consideration for Mrs. Weston's feelings. Thus when Mr. Weston invites the Eltons to join Emma's set on the outing to Box Hill, and supplies Emma with a list of reasons why this blunder was a good idea, "Emma denied none of it aloud, and agreed to none of it in private." To do otherwise "would be giving pain to his wife," something she will avoid at all costs. So, Reserved Heroine, again I say that complete openness is not in itself a good. Where concealment will prevent distress, and openness will cause it, reserve is preferable.

But pray, do not misunderstand me in this. Suppressing one's true feelings with slight evasiveness is not the same as putting on a completely false front. Between friends such outright deceit is insupportable. Frank Churchill purports to be Emma's friend, but he perpetrates an outrageous lie against her and all of Highbury society by concealing his engagement to Jane Fairfax, all the while affecting an open temper. Isabella Thorpe makes a great show of openness in speaking of her feelings to Catherine, but her confidence is all a kind of playing at openness, calculated for effect and in truth revealing nothing about her heart—except that, insofar as it exists at all, it is very false. She even goes so far as to affect an unkind reserve with her sisters, making a show of keeping a secret from them. In contrast, Catherine herself is all artlessness in her conversations, and I should like to know what, in all my novels, is more charming than her innocent self-revelations?

For while Emma's disgust with Jane Fairfax's reserve may be somewhat influenced by prejudice, Mr. Knightley also finds Jane Fairfax's reserve a fault: "She has not the open temper which a man would wish for in a wife." While Mr. Knightley's own brother John has "cool," "reserved" manners, he himself not only "love[s] an open temper"—as, I confess, do I—but has one himself, as is shown in his doing nothing mysteriously and speaking plain English. He and Emma say what they like to one another, and do not stand upon ceremony. And his never flattering Emma, but rather speaking nothing but the truth to her during all the long years before he becomes her lover, make him her truest, most valuable friend. For his openness with Emma is always in support of her improvement, and when his honesty causes her pain, it is in the great cause of teaching her where she has erred so she can make amends.

Similarly, Elinor Dashwood's reserve is all concerning matters where openness would be an evil and concealment is a good. She is very open in giving her opinion to Marianne regarding her younger sister's bad behaviour, rightly endeavouring to correct both the behaviour and the erroneous opinions upon which it is based. But she would never wound her sister's feelings merely for the pleasure of openly triumphing when the event proves her judgment to have been correct. Such self-congratulation is not the behaviour of a heroine.

My conscience tells me—before Cass or Henry do— that I have been too lenient with my Emma in my answer. Herewith my correction: Emma dislikes Jane Fairfax not so much because she disapproves of her reserve as because she is jealous of her superior accomplishments. And my heroine is not always open and artless (except where kindness and morality strictly forbid concealment), but keeps many little secrets out of self-interest or pleasure, including some from her dear Mr. Knightley. There. Now I cannot be accused of concealment myself.

In conclusion, openness can often lead to plain bad manners and an undesirable familiarity. In Marianne's case, it is a much more severe problem, causing tremendous pain and almost her own death, because a commitment to complete honesty encour- ages a dangerous spirit of self-indulgence and mili- tates against self-restraint. It is best to strike a rea- soned balance where necessary and where possible. But where the spirit is truly amiable, it is better to err on the side of openness. Even Anne Elliot herself, quieter by nature than some of my heroines, "prized the frank, the open-hearted, the eager character beyond all others."

Your signature, Reserved Heroine, tells me which of the errors, that of too much reserve or too much openness, you are in danger of falling into. Women, as I advised your sister Friendly Heroine, need com- panions of the same sex more than men do. Heroines, more than heroes, need a great deal of conversation. It is our solace and our refreshment. Excessive re- serve can interfere with the soothing balm such intimate conversation can be to an unquiet female mind. Reserve, where it is not a shield to protect the feelings of your friends, can be a wall around the heart. I shall show my friendship now by dropping my own shield and speaking to you in confidence. I have become much more guarded over the years. It is not natural for the young to be reserved, and indeed I was not. My heart was open for the world to see, and it danced as joyfully as ever heart danced in the breast of a heroine, putting on a fine show for all of Steventon to laugh at, to admire, and to applaud. Just between us—imagine that I am whispering to you now—a few of my letters escaped Cass's fire and scissors, and speak from the eighteenth century in proof of what I tell you. But to wear one's heart on one's sleeve is a fairly certain way to have it broken, you know.

Yours most faithfully,

Jane Austen

I hear Martha coming now to call me downstairs. I know my friend: she will decoy me with a lure of apple dumplings. How strange. My youth was spent in a house full of boys and men—how different from the life I now lead. I watch my sturdy, spirited little nephews and see the great men they will become. I assure you, I am their favorite aunt because I know how to talk to them, and how to treat them—as few women do. Comfortable and familiar is this house full of women, and my brothers, as you can see, are here often enough. But I do like a male presence in a house. There is something so comforting in the deep voice, so reassuring in the strong arm, so entertaining in the playful humour that teases us fretful women out of our worries. Thank goodness, here at Chawton Cottage, at least, we are all hearty souls—not a fine lady among us. No, no... You must not suspect me. You must not think I have any regrets upon that score.

Chapter Four
A Heroine in the World

*The visions of romance were over...nothing
could shortly be clearer, than that it had been
all a voluntary, self-created delusion.*
                              —Northanger Abbey

Dear Jane Austen,

Every course of study has a reading list. I was wondering, is there a reading list for heroines? What
books should a heroine-in-training read to prepare
herself for the world?

                                        Ready to Study

~~&~~

Dear Studious Heroine,

Like Emma, I could draw up a very good list of
books with which you and your sister heroines-in-
training could improve your taste, elevate your conversation, strengthen your judgment, and generally
expand your knowledge of the world. But in my por-
trayal of human behaviour I am careful to sketch
what is, not what should be. Many—dare I say
most?—of my readers are not unlike my darling
Emma and, to quote Mr. Knightley again, "will never
submit to any thing requiring industry and patience,
and a subjection of the fancy to the understanding,"
or Catherine Morland, who does "not altogether seem

particularly friendly to very severe, very intense application." These descriptions apply, at least, to heroines in their choice of pleasurable reading matter. Indeed, I might extend my discussion to include all the arts in addition to literature. So, while it would be very good for you to spend long hours studying the great paintings hanging in the grandest museums (where my own preference for men and women always causes me to attend more to the company than the sight), to sit listening to chamber orchestras with the keenest appreciation of musical composition and execution, to read Greek and Latin poetry in the original (and perhaps Shakespeare would even be considered challenging reading in your society)—nay, to translate the verses from one ancient language into another—I shall not proclaim that it is a heroine's duty to do so. While some of my heroines were deeply moved by poetry—Marianne, Anne, and Fanny were indeed— Catherine no doubt stands closer to my readers in her love of popular novels. And, like most heroines- in-training, Catherine has little use for dry history books: "The quarrels of popes and kings, with wars or pestilences, in every page; the men all so good for nothing, and hardly any women at all." It does not amaze *me*, as it does Mr. Collins (who, you will notice, never reads novels), "how little young ladies are interested by books of a serious stamp." So, treating of women as they truly are, I shall not tell you which books are the best reading for heroines-in-training. For the crux of the matter is not *what* a heroine reads, watches, or listens to, but rather with what attitude she does so.

My Catherine is, of all my heroines, the one whose reading most obviously influences her notions and her behaviour. Still, while Catherine remains in Bath, her responses to life remain "rather natural than heroic." She is largely "guided only by what was simple and probable" in her dealings even with Henry Tilney. Her responses are as innocent as she herself— who "could not tell a falsehood even to please Isabella"—is artless. Catherine's passion for reading is not merely harmless; it is positively and attractively animating, and serves as an excellent diversion from the all-consuming interest in men her friend Isabella is trying to promote. Although Henry Tilney is arousing some anxiety in her with his unexplained absence, Catherine can earnestly proclaim: "while I have Udolpho to read, I feel as if nobody could make me miserable." Yet for her at this point in the story, works of fiction are so clearly distinct from real life that Catherine's words describing dreadful events— "murder and every thing of the kind,"—"could relate only to a circulating library."

I have already begun working a little on my next novel…it is to be something quite different from anything I have yet done. I am here reminded of some lines I wrote just the other day. Let me take the pages from the drawer where they are hidden and read to you from them.... Here they are. I describe Charlotte Heywood, my heroine, thus: "sufficiently well-read in novels to supply her imagination with amusement, but not at all unreasonably influenced by them." Well, we writers all have our hobby-horses—from my first novel to my last I do not appear to escape this theme. But the influence of novels on Catherine once she reaches Northanger Abbey appears quite different. As early as her arrival upon the grounds, the look of the place "struck her as odd and inconsistent." Why? Because the Abbey does not meet the picture in her imagination, drawn from her reading in Gothic novels. To such a fervid imagination, the difference between her fancies and the reality "was very distressing." And so Catherine's time at Northanger Abbey is spent in most painfully discovering the vast gulf between imaginative visions and observed fact.

My dear Studious Heroine, almost all the books women read, from childhood's fairy tales to the popular paperback love stories of your era, contain at their core romantic narratives that women then adopt as models for real life. Thus, they attach to real people, words, actions, and even, as in Catherine's case, places, the illusions borrowed from fictional worlds.

My own girls, with some few exceptions, almost invariably misread situations because of their reliance
on imagination and wishful thinking rather than on
the objective evidence of their senses. Just as "murder and every thing of the kind" should be relished as
fiction—as sensible Henry Tilney reads *Udolpho* his
"hair standing on end the whole time,"—so too fairy-
tale romances of Prince Charmings who sweep heroines off their feet with their wealth, good looks, and
vows of eternal love can be enjoyed as fancies, but
only as such. Indeed, books are essential to a heroine's peace of mind. Emma Watson finds relief from
her great worries through "the dissipation of unpleasant ideas which only reading could produce." But you
must subject your fancy to your understanding when
you read or watch romances. Do not mistake these
illusions for reality!

> **JANE AUSTEN SAYS: A HEROINE LOVES
> ROMANTIC STORIES BUT DOES NOT
> MISTAKE THEM FOR REAL LIFE.**

Anne Elliot, the heroine of the novel I finished writing but this morning, loves romantic poetry but does
not use its sentiments to justify self-deception or self-
centeredness, as so many other romantics do. While
she enjoys discussing such works with the bereaved
Captain Benwick, she ventures to hope he does not
always read poetry, and recommends morally instruc-
tive prose to him "to rouse and fortify the mind."
Although Anne is sympathetic to Benwick's romantic
sensibility, she perceives that there is a large measure of self-indulgence in his immersion in poetry
about the wretchedness of heartbreak. Indeed, such
reading gives agony in love a pleasurable dramatic
intensity. The perceptive Anne correctly guesses that
the heartbroken young man will rally and love again.
Her romantic inclinations are the best kind, because
while thoroughly real, and thus helping to form her

sweet, sensitive nature, they never—or almost never—
blind her to reality. That is a balance few can man-
age, Studious Heroine, but it makes for a very fine
character indeed.

It is very bad when not only young ladies but
women who are old enough to know better still have
not outgrown the immature ways of the excessively
romantic, and moreover, encourage them in their
daughters. I am now thinking of Elinor and
Marianne's mother, Mrs. Dashwood. Her romantic
sensibilities create in her, as romantic sensibilities
almost always will, unwarranted expectations—as
revealed in her opinion of Edward Ferrars: "No sooner
did she perceive any symptom of love in his behaviour
to Elinor, than she considered their serious attachment as certain, and looked forward to their marriage
as rapidly approaching." And of Willoughby: she "was
led before the end of a week to hope and expect" his
marriage to Marianne. Mrs. Dashwood has passed on
this over-eagerness to one daughter, at least: "...what
Marianne and her mother conjectured one moment,
they believed the next...with them, to wish was to
hope, and to hope was to expect." In contrast, Elinor
is more like the Bath Catherine, more rational and
prudent concerning Edward's regard for her: "...till
his sentiments are fully known," she tells her romantic sister, "you cannot wonder at my wishing to avoid
any encouragement of my own partiality, by believing
or calling it more than it is." This circumspection, so
unusual in a young girl who fancies a young man, is
shown to have been wise indeed when it is discovered
that Edward has been engaged to Lucy Steele the
whole time of his acquaintance with Elinor.

Elinor wishes Marianne would be equally sensible,
but the younger girl is ruled by her fancy. Thus in
London, where she daily hopes (and so expects) to
hear from her negligent lover, she is alternately all
restless anxiety and listless melancholy. She is continually on the watch for Willoughby, so preoccupied
by this activity that she has not a moment's attention
to spare for any other. Only when her fanciful specu-

lations, rationalizations, and justifications unite to keep expectation alive is she happy. But, invariably, what her imagination creates is destroyed the next moment by facts, and "in the acuteness of the disappointment which followed such an extasy of more than hope, she felt as if, till that instant, she had never suffered." That, alas, is the painful result of unrealistic expectations. (In *The Watsons*, you know, Margaret is severely disappointed when hopes of Tom Musgrave's coming to dinner—hopes raised almost entirely by self-willed delusion and fed with elaborate preparation for the meal—are dashed. But any *disinterested* observer would have known from his uncertain response to the invitation not to expect him.)

The engaged Maria Bertram "did not want to see or understand" her situation with regard to Henry Crawford. The expected return of her father from Antigua, an event that would unite her to James Rushworth, was a gloomy prospect, and all that she could do was to throw a mist over it, and hope when the mist cleared away, she should see something else. It would hardly be *early* in November, there were generally delays, a bad passage or *something*; that favouring *something* which every body who shuts their eyes while they look, or their understandings while they reason, feels the comfort of.

Maria indeed shuts her understanding when she reasons: Henry Crawford's retaining her hand on his heart during the rehearsal of *Lovers' Vows*, even upon the announcement of Sir Thomas's return to Mansfield, "a moment of such peculiar proof and importance, was worth ages of doubt and anxiety. She hailed it as an earnest of the most serious determination..." Must I remind you, Studious Heroine, how badly things turn out for the wilfully blind, who find evidence for their desires where none exists?

Even Elinor Dashwood is led by her fondness for Edward Ferrars to rationalize:

Elinor placed all that was astonishing in [his] way of acting to his mother's account; and it was happy for

*her that he had a mother whose character was so
imperfectly known to her, as to be the general excuse
for every thing strange on the part of her son.*

No matter how many "red flags," as you might say,
could clearly be seen by an unbiased eye in Edward's
low spirits, unreserve, inconsistency, and failure to
spend time with her, to Elinor his conflict with his
mother "was the cause of all." In the absence of defi-
nite assertions, how easy it is for us to believe what it
makes us happy to believe. Mrs. Dashwood's self-
deception is more to be expected from her general
character: when Elinor protests that neither
Marianne nor Willoughby has uttered a syllable
concerning an engagement, her mother declares, "I
have not wanted syllables where actions have spoken
so plainly." Of course, there is no engagement. You
know, I believe that critics of my novels who have
been too much influenced by romanticism themselves
are afflicted with the same self-willed blindness. They
cannot see what is plain to anyone with clear vision,
and prefer to create stories that suit them rather than
read what I have written. I advise them also to take
care.

Catherine Morland's delusional expectations are
positively the result of her reading: "...the infatuation
had been created, the mischief settled long before her
quitting Bath, and it seemed as if the whole might be
traced to the influence of that sort of reading which
she had there indulged." Charlotte Heywood, on the
other hand, does not persist in her fancy when the
facts appear to contradict it, and thus she is safely
"cured...of her halfhour's fever" over Sir Edward by
what I believe you call a "reality check"—her percep-
tion of his apparent interest in another woman.

The imagination of Emma Woodhouse was also fed
by popular romantic fiction. Where else would she
have obtained fanciful notions such as those of Harriet's secret high birth or Jane Fairfax's torturous
forbidden love for Mr. Dixon (a love acquired, Emma
speculates luridly, by Jane's "sucking in the sad
poison")? Poor Emma is again and again confronted

with her errors, as here when she looks back at her mistaken conviction that Mr. Elton had a romantic interest in Harriet: "She had taken up the idea, she supposed, and made every thing bend to it." Such is the way with imaginists, even such clever ones as Emma Woodhouse.

> **JANE AUSTEN SAYS: A HEROINE FOUNDS HER EXPECTATIONS ON FACTS AND COMMON SENSE, NOT FANTASY AND WISHFUL THINKING.**

Perhaps by now you are thinking of the words of that famous twentieth-century writer, Mr. Ernest Hemingway: "...swell advice. Try and take it some-time." (Such unnatural characters! Did anyone on God's earth ever speak as they do? No woman ever did, I shall vouch for it.) Well, I grant you this: per-haps Charlotte Heywood is rather too sober-minded for a heroine. And there is certainly a great deal to admire in Marianne's ardent eagerness and unre-serve. To be driven almost wild by poetry—who would wish to dampen such enthusiasm? Her response to drawings, and to the beautiful natural world that inspires both drawings and poems is never less than rapturous delight and admiration. That is indeed the proper response to books and all forms of art, Studi-ous Heroine. But I must insist that you not confuse novels with life—no novels, that is, except my own.

Yours ever,

Jane Austen

~~&~~

Dear Jane Austen,

I live in New York City and every day I just want to punch someone out. I mean, people stop to dial their cell phones in the most inconvenient places—in the middle of crosswalks, halfway up the subway steps. In Regency terms, it's as if they took out their quill pens and a sheet of paper in the middle of the High Street and started writing a note to Aunt Sally there in the road, causing people behind to jostle each other in the attempt to come to a halt in time and neither trample nor be trampled by other pedestrians or horses. But this is worse because they proceed to shout the most deeply banal things you can imagine (think Mrs. Allen, Miss Bates, Mrs. Bennet) for all the world to hear. And I can't go to the ATM—that's a cash machine in the vestibule of the bank—because some homeless person is camped out there. And the shopkeepers are so rude! And men, in particular, so vulgar, spreading their legs so they take up two seats on the subway! I feel as if I'm going to blow a gasket. Is it any better in the country? I am really beginning to hate people and I want to know: is that an okay thing for a heroine to do?

A Misanthrope

~~&~~

Dear Misanthropic Heroine,

Please sit down and pour yourself a glass of Con-stantia wine before your swelling heart bursts with anger. Perhaps you will not believe it, but I have been accused of hating people myself, not least because of a few sharp lines in my letters. Little did I know when I had Anne Elliot express my view that no one ought to be judged by the testimony of personal letters— that "no private correspondence could bear the eye of others"— that I would be condemned by many for private remarks of my own. Even a writer who I dare say studied my novels faithfully and learned quite a lot about the art of fiction from them, one Mr. E. M. Forster, pronounced that one hears "the whinneying of harpies" in my words to Cass, a little joke about a neighbor that I certainly never imagined would be read by any other than its intended recipient. (And yet, dearest Cass has been castigated by posterity for burning most of my correspondence and cutting out portions of those letters she passed on as keep-sakes—acts for which it will take all eternity for me to thank her!) At least one critic made a name for him-self in the twentieth century by examining what he called my "hatred" of people. So I have not been immune to charges of misanthropy myself. And in-deed, I have sometimes felt that I did not want people to be agreeable, as that saved me the trouble of liking them a great deal. But except where such harsh judgments of your neighbors as you express will serve to do some good—and even the reward of amusement is not sufficient reason if it causes pain to another or feeds your own bitterness—you must not succumb to them.

There is a certain kind of self-absorption—we are all absorbed in ourselves to some degree, of course—I mean a measure beyond the ordinary—that threatens to destroy the foundations of common civility. I am afraid the romantic elevation of individual desire over the general welfare has fostered this unfortunate development. Thus, the gentleman stops in the most inconvenient of places to dial his cell phone, putting his own ease over the common good without so much as a second thought. (Marianne, you will recall, would never submit to adjusting her words or behaviour the slightest degree in the name of courtesy, and you will find many other characters in my novels with the same attitude.) You are quite right to deplore his behaviour but do not let it affect you so strongly. Such sensitivity will ruin your happiness—heroines should be made of sterner stuff, or if not, then they must choose to behave as though they were.

Now, the examples you give are instances of rather minor incivility—though to be sure they are sufficient to corrode the veneer of civilization until it is nearly ruined (I beg your pardon—I daresay Adam met with that analogy in the first novel he opened). But such a lack of consideration often extends to more important matters. Willoughby's ruling principle is selfishness, you will recall, but so too is Marianne's. Thus, with

no fixed principles to guide her, but relying on the
vagaries of egotism entirely, she is "neither reasonable nor candid": "She expected from other people the
same opinions and feelings as her own, and she
judged of their motives by the immediate effects of
their actions on herself." Since the lovers both decide
about others on the strength of their powerful imagi-
nations rather than observation, their assessments
are invariably "prejudiced and unjust." So, dear
Misanthropic Heroine, while you are correct in condemning the nearly universal triumph of selfishness
as the determinant of behaviour in your city, do not
fall into the error of taking such behaviour as a personal affront, thereby indulging in a sort of vanity of
indignation yourself. Bid adieu to disappointment
and spleen, I beg you. For the *effects* of others' actions do not always reveal their *motives,* strong as is
the temptation to believe they do, and for this reason
candour—which Marianne lacks—is a most desirable
trait for a heroine. Indeed, some of my girls must
acquire it before they can attain their happy endings.

As I very likely have a different understanding of the
word candour than you do, I shall elaborate. Jane
Bennet's "mild and steady candour" is described this
way by her sister Elizabeth: "without ostentation or
design—to take the good of every body's character
and make it still better, and say nothing of the bad."
Let us agree to go by that definition. Jane urges
Elizabeth for her own sake to judge others more
generously also, and it would have been better for her
if she had listened to the advice, for Jane is shown to
be right in several instances in her defense of the
motives of others, most importantly in the case of Mr.
Darcy.

Emma Woodhouse also judges others rather
harshly, frequently basing her views, as Marianne
does, on the strength of fancy rather than observation. (By the bye, as in Elizabeth's case, the result is
often some rather fine wit, which does not excuse the
behaviour.) Yet *favourable* judgments decided in the
same careless way are also often mistaken, and as we

see in many cases with my girls, when such views lead to precipitate *action*—and not merely Jane Bennet's open mind—can cause problems as well. Observe that the same three heroines err on both sides of the matter.

Although Jane Bennet is not the heroine of *Pride and Prejudice*, she has something to teach her sister about the way a heroine should judge the behaviour of others. Elizabeth has just indicated that her opinion of Mr. Bingley's character has been sunk because Jane has been hurt by his apparent change of heart regarding her. Jane replies:

"We must not be so ready to fancy ourselves intentionally injured. We must not expect a lively young man to be always so guarded and circumspect. It is very often nothing but our own vanity that deceives us. Women fancy admiration means more than it does."

"And men take care that they should."

"If it is designedly done, they cannot be justified; but I have no idea of there being so much design in the world as some persons imagine."

Elizabeth goes on to say, quite rightly, that thoughtlessness and carelessness can cause as much misery as design. While she is correct, Jane's willingness to believe the best of others, and to forgive unintended injuries is by far the better course. For when we judge the actions of others solely by their effects upon ourselves, we frequently have a false or incomplete understanding of the circumstances. Rather, give others the benefit of the doubt and assume their motives are innocent unless and until good sense directs you to do otherwise. Particularly when weighing the behaviour of the male sex, do not fall into the error of believing men act with the consciousness and penetration of females in matters of the heart.

Young Catherine Morland has something to teach her sister heroines on this point. When Henry Tilney greets Catherine with cool reserve after a misunderstanding:

Feelings rather natural than heroic possessed her; instead of considering her own dignity injured by this ready condemnation—instead of proudly resolving, in conscious innocence, to shew her resentment towards him who could harbour a doubt of it, to leave to him all the trouble of seeking an explanation, and to enlighten him on the past only by avoiding his sight, or flirting with somebody else, she took to herself all the shame of misconduct, or at of least its appearance, and was only eager for an opportunity of explaining its cause.

Women are so very quick to resent men's behaviour that they help to create mutual distrust and unease. In contrast, Catherine's warmth here effects what heroic ice never could: she melts Henry's reserve in an instant.

I should also like to urge you to have a more open mind, and a more compassionate heart, where the poor are concerned. It is not by *design* that they inconvenience you so greatly. Do you think the beggar at the bank would be there to distress you if he had anywhere else to go? Here at Chawton Cottage we try to do our part by making clothing for the poor and teaching their children to read. You should spend more time considering how you might relieve the distress of others, and less time dwelling on how others are injuring you—for your own sake as well as theirs.

However, I must say, dear Misanthropic Heroine, that I am quite of your mind about the city. Living there, I believe, one gets the worst impressions of human nature. Elinor Dashwood's rule of "general civility," so scorned by Marianne, is not much in evidence. When my family moved from the country to Bath I found myself exposed to such disgusting and at the same time tedious spectacles of that nature that I simply could not continue to find people agreeable. You know, I got almost no writing done in the city: I left off for nearly ten full years in between those happier times when I lived in the country. You may indeed find that you like people better when you, and they, are away from the smoke, dirt, noise, and endless Vanity Fair of the city.

Yours,

Jane Austen

JANE AUSTEN SAYS: A HEROINE DOES NOT JUDGE THE MOTIVES OF OTHERS BY THE EFFECTS OF THEIR ACTIONS UPON HERSELF.

I hear a carriage arriving. It must bring my dear brother Edward. Sweet, beautiful Edward—I shudder to think where I should be without him. His generosity to his poor sisters and mother in giving us this cottage to live in can never be repaid with sufficient gratitude. Do you happen to know Edward's story? It is not to be credited as truth, and yet it is such. Mr. and Mrs. Knight—the dear lady, my only patroness—had no children and a great deal of money. My father and mother had many sons. The Knights—our distant cousins—took a fancy to Edward when he was quite young. (If you can believe it, they took him along on their wedding tour!) They later adopted him, and he is now the heir to a very great fortune and lives at Godmersham, the grandest of houses, with a splendid park—far surpassing Mr. Darcy's Pemberley. If you read his story you would say it was too far out of the common way to be found anywhere but in a novel. How unlikely, that a wealthy, landowning family should adopt a boy whose parents were alive and quite able to support him comfortably. However, it is true, thank goodness, for the sake of his family. (Edward's good fortune has certainly been good fortune for all.) A romantic story out of a novel and yet quite, quite true.

I must go down to greet my brother, and see how goes the life in luxurious East Kent.

Chapter Five
A Heroine Knows a Hero When She Sees One—Or Does She?

> *His person and air were equal to what her fancy had ever drawn for the hero of a favourite story...*
>
> —*Sense and Sensibility*

Dear Jane Austen,

I am a forty-five-year-old-woman who wants to get married. I recently met someone named Tom (GQbeachmogul) on an Internet dating site. We met for drinks and I thought things were going well. He reached across the table and held my hand during our second drink. At the end of the date he said, "So, you'll let me know what you think?" At the time I didn't think he could have meant that but when I didn't hear from him after a week I reconsidered and e-mailed him. I read somewhere that men consider first dates job interviews. So, I figured he was waiting to hear from Human Resources. He said he was delighted I had gotten in touch. We went out on a second date, and, um, we got drunk and made out at the bar. He called the next morning, which in my experience definitely means STRONG INTEREST. Then I went away on a 5-day trip. We exchanged more e-mails when I returned (I wrote first) but didn't go out again. Now it's been two weeks and I haven't heard from him. Telepathic messages do not seem to be working. Dear Jane, what happened? And can I call him to find out? Is it possible that he doesn't know I like him? He really seemed to like me. Maybe he doesn't know I like him and has to hear it from me. But I don't want to chase him! What should I do? Can I call him?

Spinning My Wheels

~~&~~

Dear Spinning Heroine,

I fear you have run your curricle into a muddy ditch. You have spent two intimate evenings with Mr. GQ and you suspect that had you gained his affection on those occasions he would by now have found the means necessary to make you aware of his sentiments. You wonder if he is restrained from revealing his interest by diffidence, let us say. Perhaps you compare your problem to the one Jane Bennet's placid manner caused her, as you will remember from this conversation between Charlotte Lucas and Lizzy Bennet:

"...it is sometimes a disadvantage to be so very guarded. If a woman conceals her affection with the same skill from the object of it, she may lose the opportunity of fixing him...there are very few of us who have heart enough to be really in love without encouragement.... Bingley likes your sister undoubtedly; but he may never do more than like her, if she does not help him on."

"But she does help him on, as much as her nature will allow. If *I* can perceive her regard for him, he must be a simpleton indeed not to discover it too."

Pray, do not take Charlotte's incisive commentary as license for your own decision to "help on" this man. It is true that Elizabeth, clever as she is, overlooks the fact that men are largely clueless (a fine new word, by the bye) about women's feelings. Bingley does not in fact discover the depth of Jane's regard for him until the end of the novel. And heroes sometimes do require encouragement, which my heroines are advised to supply. (Edmund Bertram wonders at Crawford's perseverance with Fanny: "he did not think he could have gone on himself with any woman breathing, without something more to warm his courage than his eyes could discern in hers.") But Jane was also the picture of modesty and propriety and hid her feelings well—perhaps too well. You, on the other hand, have been shockingly profligate: you let GQ hold your hand; you drank like a fishmonger's wife; you exposed yourself with him at a public house; you brazenly initiated contact with the gentleman (if I may so call him) more than once. You have given him encouragement enough! There is no telling yet whether or not his attentions to you were sincere; but your part now is simply to wait until he makes his intentions apparent. I am aware that precipitateness is all the fashion, but you must learn patience and restraint. And pray, in the future, confine your behaviour with this suitor to more ladylike activities—at the very least until he has declared himself. As your signature suggests, desperate activity, however vigorous, does not always bring one nearer the goal. And desperation will almost certainly be repugnant to the true hero you seek to attract.

I remain yours very faithfully,

Jane Austen

JANE AUSTEN SAYS: A HEROINE NEVER PURSUES A HERO.

How I am besieged with questions from women who share that terrible affliction: an attraction to men whom they term "bad boys." This putrid infection is epidemic and fatal to happiness. If you have caught it, Reader, neither embrocations nor the sea air, hartshorn nor Constantia wine will be of use in effecting a cure. But do not despair; relief is possible. If you truly have the will to recover, read on for my receipt.

Dear Jane Austen,

I am always attracted to "bad boys" who break my heart. I am in love with one right now. Why, oh why, are women always attracted to that type?

Suffering

~~&~~

Dear Suffering Heroine,

You exhibit the classic symptoms of having read too many romances and watched too many Hollywood movies. Think what you are about—and what they are about. Is there a trace of the real, the true, the everyday in them? I should not be surprised to learn that you swooned over Heathcliff. (*Quelle horreur*! as my dear sister Eliza used to exclaim.) Earth to Suffering Heroine (as incredulity and exasperation might induce one of your era to say): *the man hangs puppies just for fun*! But, to be sure, most "bad boys" are not murderous lunatics howling on the moors. Many, indeed, are utterly charming. Some win your presidential elections. But none, you may have noticed, win the hands of my heroines.

I have attended a sufficient number of balls at enough watering-places to have observed that bad boys come in many varieties. (You might not believe it to look at me now, but there were nights when I had a partner for every dance.) A fine example in my novels is Willoughby, the dashing Byron-like figure who wins Marianne's heart—for a time—in *Sense and Sensibility*. Like you, Marianne is a romantic dreamer with a mind saturated in love stories. Upon meeting Willoughby she thinks (as the epigraph to this chapter says), "His person and air were equal to what her fancy had ever drawn for the hero of a favourite story..." In his looks, his spirits, his abilities, his tastes, "[h]e was exactly formed to engage Marianne's heart" and she gives it to him almost upon meeting him. What is amiss in this picture? She fancies him a hero because he resembles her fantasy of a hero!

Marianne's is but another self-created delusion. (Does this sound at all familiar, my Suffering Heroine?) True, the extent of Willoughby's villainy is well concealed at this point but even here there are signs of a bad character that Marianne refuses to read. Worse yet, she converts his flaws into *good, attractive* traits and she mirrors them most energetically. Her wiser sister Elinor notes disapprovingly that Willoughby speaks his mind too openly "without attention to persons or circumstances." He is rude, unjust, incautious, and indecorous—not the characteristics one would think suitable for a hero. Yet, such is human perversity that the appearance of these qualities in a handsome, lively, engaging young man who has set out to ensnare a young lady in training for a heroine often increases his attraction. To a susceptible mind—like Marianne's—like yours?—they confer upon him the exciting status of a rebel, a flouter of social strictures and boring rules. Because her values have been warped by her reading (or, I suspect, moviegoing in your case), he gives her the tremulous thrill (the "rush") that a true gentleman cannot. And once Marianne has fallen in love with her own creation, she is unshakeable and even her lover's hardness towards her in breaking things off—he is cruel, insulting, remorseless, mercenary, cowardly—cannot kill her passion for him. The blackest opium dens hidden down the darkest alleys in Cheapside do not boast truer addicts than lovers like Marianne! She almost dies—in wilful self-destruction—not over a flesh-and-blood man but over a dream of a hero.

My dear Suffering Heroine, in my role as apothecary, I entreat you to read my novel again. Yes, read it. Do not under any circumstances believe that the Hollywood movie, in which Gothic romance is brought in by the scullery door and fantasies encouraged where they should be exploded, will effect the same cure. If the life of lovers consisted of nothing but reading Cowper's poetry, quizzing neighbors, and dancing reels, all the while looking a charming couple, Willoughby might just make a sufficient hero. Since it does not, I leave it to you to determine if a thoroughly selfish and heartless coward makes the grade.

Yours very faithfully,

Jane Austen

The coach is late today. No doubt this wretched weather has slowed its pace. I must include some clever remarks about the storm in my next reply, for I have observed that if one writes about the weather in a letter, it is generally completely changed before the letter is read. My mother is surely impatient to be in the garden but upon consideration this enforced captivity just suits my aching joints. Now, what new lament have we here?

Dear Jane Austen,

I am in love with a guy who cheats on me. He gets a thrill out of putting notches on the old belt. He hits on barmaids and personal trainers, his colleagues and mine. He's asked out my friends, even my sister! I can't imagine life without him but I couldn't go on this way for the rest of my life. Tell me, you who see into everyone's hearts, can such men ever be re-formed?

Heartbroken but Hopeful

~~&~~

Dear Heartbroken Heroine,

You like this collector of hearts, do you? Would you suffer more if he were a collector of scalps such as were once found amongst the native tribes of North America? Surely you recognize your lover in the character of Henry Crawford in *Mansfield Park*. (I hear you murmuring in protest against references to examples in *Mansfield Park*. Another reader who throws down the book in disgust because Fanny Price is not Elizabeth Bennet. But there are as many styles as there are heroines, I assure you, and you can learn a lot from the way that little wisp of a thing deals with

Henry Crawford. I hope I am not so dull an artist as to paint the same picture again and again.)

Henry is one of those men—short, plain, decidedly not handsome—who easily wins the hearts of women through the force of sheer charm. Witty, intelligent, confident, playful, interesting, and rather well off, he would be ashamed to rely on mere good looks to ensure conquests. Although he does not share Willoughby's personal attraction, he does share his ruling principle of selfishness. Purely to gratify his ego, Henry delights in making both Maria and Julia Bertram fall in love with him, a particularly dastardly act in its compound disregard for the relationship between the sisters and for that between Maria and her betrothed, James Rushworth. (True, Rushworth would stand a fair chance—how might you express it?—of losing a caterpillar-herding contest to Ozzy Osbourne, nonetheless Maria had eyes and she chose him.) Far from discouraging Crawford, both of these circumstances rather increase his pleasure in the dalliance. (Jane Bennet's candour would have her point out in his defense that "...he began with no object but of making them like him. He did not want them to die of love..." And her sister Elizabeth would indignantly retort that "...with sense and temper which ought to have made him judge and feel better, he allowed himself great latitude on such points.")

Henry loves a challenge, so he is intrigued by Fanny's lack of interest and outright rebuffs, and he becomes determined to sport with her affections in the same manner as he does with those of his richer, easier prey:

...her not loving him now was scarcely regretted. A little difficulty to be overcome, was no evil to Henry Crawford. He rather derived spirits from it. He had been apt to gain hearts too easily. His situation was new and animating.

Let me point out *en passant* that in this love of a challenge Henry is rather more typical of man than not, just as he is typical in that he "can never bear to ask" for directions when he is lost. (Here let me digress for a moment to say that I very much regret having left my novel *The Watsons* unfinished, but it was begun during a bad time for me. My dear, affectionate father, you know, who had such faith in my genius...well, never mind. But it contains some of my finest writing as well as another excellent illustration of my point here. Emma Watson also piques the interest of several fine gentlemen by artlessly, not coquettishly, rebuffing their advances.) It is only the element of deliberate cruelty in Henry's design that makes it wrong. And, despite "some previous ill-opinion" of him on Fanny's part, so good is Henry Crawford at gaining hearts that he might have ensnared Fanny's had it not been long and securely Edmund's. In the event—and here I entreat you to pay particular attention because this is where your reformation question comes in—Fanny rather wins *his* heart without making any effort to do so—on the contrary, she unfailingly discourages him—and he consequently determines not only to conquer but to marry her.

Some of my readers are shocked when they read that Fanny would indeed have been his ultimate reward if he had persevered, but so it is. I do not write of human feelings and behaviour as they should be but as they are:

Could he have been satisfied with the conquest of one amiable woman's affections, could he have found sufficient exultation in overcoming the reluctance, in working himself into the esteem and tenderness of Fanny Price, there would have been every probability of success and felicity for him.

But Fanny showed no signs yet of such melting and, thus discouraged by his first choice, when Henry saw Maria again "...the temptation of immediate pleasure was too strong for a mind unused to make any sacrifice to right..." So, with the strongest incentive in the world to reform, Henry Crawford ultimately could not. Such men do not represent promising prospects for heroines. They are self-indulgent, vain, and grandiose. Their egotism knows no bounds. As a rule they feel quite assured of the success of their amorous endeavours. Elizabeth Bennet is properly ashamed that her earlier encouraging behaviour to Wickham contributed to this natural self-assurance: he is secure in the belief that "...however long, and for whatever cause, his attentions had been withdrawn, her vanity would be gratified and her preference secured at any time by their renewal."

Now to your question—or, rather, what should have been your question: can *you* reform such a man? If you are attracted to those qualities that mark him as a rake—and you evidently are (especially if that is your usual "type")—then I am very sorry to break the news that you do not have the character required to reform him. Fanny admired only Henry Crawford's good qualities. His faults were, to use one of your era's expressions, deal-breakingly repulsive to her. You, on the other hand, must admire the rakish traits or you would not as a rule favor men who possessed them to begin with. It is by far the most prudent course to encourage the attentions of good men and refuse to countenance those of any others, declining courteously the offers of such unsuitable men as seek to attach you, but in such a manner as to leave no doubt of your firmness.

And now, having written so much on one side of the question, I shall turn round and make some further discriminating remarks. There are degrees of badness. Mr. Wickham and William Elliot—from *Persuasion*—are quite bad. They are mercenary, false, vicious, and immoral, like Willoughby. But they share some traits with a man who is merely careless and thoughtless, selfish but not wicked, and that is Frank Churchill. One attribute they share is a "well-bred ease of manner" that makes them favourites in society. "Emma was directly sure that [Frank Churchill] knew how to make himself agreeable.... He understood what would be welcome..." My readers naturally fall for these charmers, some of whom, like Henry Crawford, can be kind and generous when it suits them, as well as charming. (I cannot tell you how many in my own family wanted me to let Fanny marry him!) Even sensible Elinor, after all Willoughby has done to hurt a most beloved sister, falls under Willoughby's spell when she is in his presence—and for some time thereafter: "...his influence over her mind was heightened by circumstances which ought not in reason to have weight; by that person of un-common attraction, [and] that open, affectionate, and lively manner which it was no merit to possess." Elizabeth Bennet comes to understand how she could have mistaken Wickham's character so completely: "His countenance, voice, and manner, had estab-lished him at once in the possession of every virtue." But in all cases this ease of manner is not real open-ness. These men are all hiding secrets, using their charm to trick women, to "get over," as you say.

Now, Frank is a favorite of mine and I can forgive his faults because he is so very funny and spirited. I arrange for him to be happy but I could not reward him with my Emma, now could I? Mr. Knightley may not have Frank's youthful high spirits and playful-ness, but he will never hurt Emma the way Frank has hurt Jane Fairfax. Can you doubt that she will suffer still more from his impulsive, careless, selfish ways once they are married, despite his best intentions? Emma quite justly censures his behaviour, which falls short of the correct standards for a man in having: "None of that upright integrity, that strict adherence to truth and principle, that disdain of trick and littleness, which a man should display in every transaction of his life." But if you truly rank the enjoyment of a lively spirit and quick though occa-sionally improper wit as a greater good than peace of mind; if you would find Mr. Knightley a deadly bore with his rectitude and his lectures, and Colonel Brandon an old stick-in-the-mud, and would prefer to these paragons of virtue a man who might surprise you by proposing an excursion to a pleasant resort such as Weymouth

—Good heavens, Henry! You quite made me jump out of my skin! How long have you been reading over my shoulder? What's that?

My cosmopolitan brother informs me that Las Vegas would be a more appropriate example—or Las Vegas, then, the very weekend he had arranged to meet with his architect to discuss improvements to your estate—perhaps the design of that elegant bow window you have desired for years; or one who would make extravagant gestures as when Willoughby gives Marianne a horse that, romantic and delightful a gift as it is, cannot ultimately be accepted because it would be too expensive for her mother to keep, or when Frank bestows on Jane the pianofortè that brings her nearly as much pain as pleasure—then you might try your luck reforming not a bad boy like Bill Clinton or Tommy Lee, but a slightly naughty one. Yes, like you, Henry. Insufferable man, he is proud of it! But, if you please, do not in future protest that you were not warned of the heartache.

Your very sincere friend,

Jane Austen

> **JANE AUSTEN SAYS: A HEROINE WOULD SOONER SIT DOWN TO A SUPPER OF THIN GRUEL THAN GIVE HER HEART TO A BAD BOY.**

Now I've offended my favorite brother and the dear fellow has gone off to work his charm on the rest of the household. What a Henry!

Dear Jane Austen,

A few months ago I started seeing Mike. At first I wasn't very interested and he really had to pursue me. He took me to nice restaurants, wouldn't think of letting me pay for anything, complimented me a lot, even took me away for weekends. I started falling in love with him so I thought we were on the same page, wanting to be together all the time. I moved some things into his apartment, bought him nice presents. Now I'm completely hooked. But over the past few weeks I've sensed him cooling towards me. Little things I do seem to irritate him. He is not calling me or making plans to see me as often as he used to. Well, last night he found out he would be laid off in two weeks. I am in a position to lend him money and introduce him to potential employers. Should I offer to help him out? I think that might rekindle his interest in me because he would see how much I cared.

Hesitant

~~&~~

Dear Hesitant Heroine,

Let me attempt to spare you some of the suffering my heroines endure when they look back at their experiences and all at once are struck with the foolishness of their behaviour. Consider your history with Mike. When did he desire you, treat you well, try to please you, in short, appear to love you ardently? When you were elusive. Men today are all like Henry Crawford in being apt to win hearts too easily. Has it escaped your notice that Mike was happiest when he was exerting himself to win you? Withdraw some distance and allow him once more the space through which to pursue you. You have already displayed "too masculine and bold a temper," such as Penelope Watson revealed when she pursued rich old Dr. Harding. To offer your beau financial assistance would aggravate your problem, not ameliorate it. Your situation recalls to my mind Mr. Darcy's behaviour. Pay close attention to what I am about to tell you and its relevance to your situation will become clear.

You will recollect that Elizabeth did not find Darcy attractive when he was cold and superior, for all his large fortune and good looks. She found his bad

behaviour insufferable (bad boy lovers take note) and
so refused an offer of marriage from one of the most
eligible men in England—one made, incidentally, with
the same smug security we have seen in the manner
of bad boys once they have determined to attach a
woman. (I myself once turned down a proposal of
marriage from a most attractive suitor. That is, I
accepted Harris and then passed a sleepless night
and the next morning...oh, dear, even now the memory distresses me. A most painful reversal...unavoid-
able with such feelings as mine and yet...Where was
I? Oh, yes...to be sure, Mr. Darcy.) Was he put off,
even by a particularly cruel and insulting rejection—
"with so little *endeavour* at civility" on Elizabeth's
part? On the contrary, her words "tortured" him and
over time he only hoped "to lessen [her] ill-opinion, by
letting [her] see that [her] reproofs had been attended
to." No effort was too great in his quest to win Elizabeth's approval. He changed his behaviour and, to
borrow Spinning Heroine's analogy, applied again for
the same position as her husband much later. (Much
as my brother Henry did with poor Cousin Eliza after
she turned him down. How I miss her!)

Elizabeth tells Jane that she can date her love for
Darcy to her "first seeing his beautiful grounds at
Pemberley," and it is a very good joke, but he truly
begins to attach her when she realizes there that he
is very different both from the man he was and the
man she took him to be. He is, in fact, worthy of her.
Darcy's treatment of Elizabeth and her aunt and
uncle is astonishingly kind, polite, good-tempered,
and generous, and his housekeeper informs Elizabeth
that such is his behaviour to all within his circle,
servants and poor included. Here Elizabeth is driven
to reexamine her feelings towards him. She acknowledges esteem, respect, gratitude, and interest but she
is unsure if she also feels love. Notice that all these
good feelings, which do not arise until they are
earned, precede and inspire her feelings of love. Darcy
does not stop there in his treatment of Elizabeth as a
priceless treasure: he hunts down Wickham and
Lydia and bribes the scoundrel to marry her, thus

ensuring a sworn enemy as his brother should he succeed with Elizabeth. He tries to keep this noble act a secret, evidence he has acted out of pure consideration, not the desire to be rewarded. Now, here is the part most relevant to your situation, my Hesitant Heroine: all of these chivalrous services not only make Elizabeth fall in love with him: they make him fall even more passionately and selflessly in love with her. You see, it is a curious truth that the way you treat someone can determine how you feel about that person. (Mrs. Norris, of *Mansfield Park*, "disliked Fanny, because she had neglected her...") All that is required of Elizabeth is that she receive Darcy's services graciously. She does. His actions inspire the precise response in her that fans the fire of his interest: her sincere expression of deep gratitude is immediately followed by a renewal of his profession of love, a second proposal, this one, of course, to be accepted.

> **JANE AUSTEN SAYS: A HEROINE GRACIOUSLY RECEIVES A HERO'S SERVICES.**

When Edmund Bertram, in the kindest way, helps his meek little ten-year-old cousin Fanny write a letter to her brother William,

...[her] feelings...were such as she believed herself incapable of expressing; but her countenance and a few artless words fully conveyed all their gratitude and delight, and her cousin began to find her an interesting object.

Notice that once again the heroine's gratitude for the hero's services arouses his interest in her.

My letter grows long indeed, yet this point is worth dwelling on, for twenty-first-century heroines simply do not understand it. Mr. Knightley is similarly selfless in his desire to be of service to Emma. He does not let his strong jealousy of Frank Churchill ultimately interfere with his desire to see Emma happy, at whatever cost to himself. And after he has won the promise of Emma's hand in marriage he finds a way to perform a yet more extraordinary service: because doing so will ease her mind about her father, he agrees to move from his own house to hers, one he will share with a most tedious father-in-law—one evil, at least, that I have gratefully escaped. (As Mrs. Weston notes of Mr. Knightley in a further illustration of his excellent promise as a domestic mate, "Little things do not irritate him.") A better present than a distressing pianoforté or unacceptable horse! Those only cost money. Compare such paltry gifts to Colonel Brandon's inestimable helpfulness when Marianne is ill, particularly in riding off to fetch Mrs. Dashwood, to which Elinor's response, as I recall very well, is this:

> *The comfort of such a friend at that moment as Colonel Brandon—of such a companion for her mother,—how gratefully was it felt!—a companion whose judgment would guide, whose attendance must relieve, and whose friendship might sooth her!—as far as the shock of such a summons could be lessened to her, his presence, his manners, his assistance, would lessen it.*

His desire to serve Marianne comprehends her family, and so he finds a way to please Elinor by offering employment to Edward Ferrars. When Marianne recovers from her illness, Brandon stays the course by helping her through her convalescence. To give these gifts to her makes him happy. By the time he wins Marianne's hand he has worked very hard to earn it, and that makes her especially precious to him. If selfishness is Willoughby's ruling principle, the desire to serve his beloved is Colonel Brandon's.

JANE AUSTEN SAYS: A HEROINE DOES NOT TRY TO WIN A HERO'S LOVE.

Now the subject of Elinor and Edward has arisen, I must pause over it. Many readers are of the opinion that Edward Ferrars is not quite worthy of Elinor Dashwood. I believe this disapprobation is not unconnected with his passive temperament. We find Elinor assisting him more frequently than he expends effort on her behalf. She endeavours to relieve the distress and discomfort that arise from his ill-considered engagement to Lucy Steele, though she herself is grieved by the attachment. Edward does little for Elinor beyond proposing to her once he is honorably released from his engagement. It is rather Colonel Brandon who acts decisively and forcefully on her behalf. Thus, because Colonel Brandon acts in her interest when he offers the living of Delaford to Edward, she appears in the role of the latter's benefactress. There is no doubt something wrong in this arrangement. The more energy Elinor expends, the more passive she makes Edward, with the sorry result that he appears not masculine or bold enough. (Do not confuse my Edward with that attractive but rather nervous fellow who played the role in the last decade of the twentieth century. Lou—no, Hugh...a quite shocking rumor about him has reached my ears.... I fear there is madness in his bloodline...but I digress.) Upon reflection, I am persuaded that for this very reason their romance does not have the solid, conclusive feeling of rightness that Mr. Darcy's and Elizabeth's does.

Are you not yet convinced? If you desire further evidence I ask you to consider: when does Frank Churchill ask his adoptive father's permission to marry Jane Fairfax? Not while he is allowing her to stoop to the uncomfortable and improper position of conducting a secret engagement. During that long period of duplicity he takes her for granted and mistreats her. It is only after she breaks with him, returns his letters, and accepts a position as a governess that he is roused to behave with the decisiveness and quickness of a true lover. (All this happens only after his aunt's death, to be sure. Mr. Woodhouse blunders into a truth when he complains that Frank

Churchill is "not quite the thing." Stay; I fear I have quoted that line before. Forgive me. I am becoming Miss Bates, tiresome old chatterbox, repeating my own nonsense and trying the patience of my listeners.) Once Frank fears that he has lost Jane forever, the activities, physical and otherwise, entailed in winning her back elevate his spirits to great heights and he becomes almost deliriously happy in his success.

I offer you a further example in illustration of my point: Henry Tilney is not troubled by the least doubt of Catherine Morland's regard for him. He is perfectly aware that her heart is securely his. Yet he similarly draws energy from those situations near the end of *Northanger Abbey* (as you know it, though I gave my novel different names at various points) in which he is stirred from his comfortable role as charming wit (Are all Henrys thus?) to act heroically on her behalf. The more he is able to relieve her distress, the more he loves her. First, he comforts her after her dreadful suspicions against his father are exposed and later, when he and Catherine are sundered by both physical distance and his father's express opposition to their union, he hastens to Fullerton like a hero of romance to propose to her. And as for that other Henry, nothing thrills and delights the worldly Mr. Crawford more than the service he performs for Fanny in using his influence to see that her brother William is promoted to the rank of Lieutenant— except, perhaps, his observation of the effect this intelligence has on her face, her words, her heart.

Captain Harville, a serious man in a soberer novel than either *Northanger Abbey* or *Emma* (in these lines I have just decided to add to this new scene—they are rather good, do not you think?), attempts to paint for Anne Elliot this picture of men's desire to *act* on behalf of their wives and children: "If I could explain to you...all that a man can bear and do, and glories to do for the sake of these treasures of his existence!" So, my Hesitant Heroine, do not usurp Mike's masculine role. Rather, simply stand back and allow him to do what he glories to do and he will love you for it.

Yours most faithfully,

Jane Austen

JANE AUSTEN SAYS: A HEROINE ALLOWS A HERO THE EXCITEMENT OF WINNING HER LOVE.

Dear Jane Austen,

I was out at a cigar bar tonight and from across the room I spotted a very cute guy smoking a large cigar. I felt instantly crazy about him and I found out from the bartender that he was a regular, which is great because it means I can find him there again. He smiled at me and said hello when he walked by on his way out. I'm in love! Tell me, dear Miss Austen, do you believe in love at first sight?

Lovestruck

~~&~~

Dear Lovestruck Heroine,

Oh, well I know the delightful, giddy experience you describe. I was only fifteen when I gave the same sensations to my heroine Laura in *Love and Freindship* (yes, that is how I spelled it): "...no sooner did I first behold [the stranger], than I felt that on him the happiness or Misery of my future Life must depend." But, *hello*— I was joking! I half suspect you must be in liquor to make such an inquiry in all seriousness. Upon my word, it is extraordinary how often bad boys—including the ones discussed above—make remarkably good first impressions. Now, as a good child of the eighteenth century—The Age of Reason, you know—I would not want to lead you astray with false logic. It does not follow that because bad boys make good first impressions, all who make good first impressions must therefore be bad. The excellent impression made by Henry Tilney upon Catherine's first meeting him is not diminished by her better knowledge of the gentleman. But the frequency with which those early favourable views are reversed should make you hesitate to trust first impressions until they are confirmed by further experience.

First Impressions. Did you know that was my original title for *Pride and Prejudice*? For sensible Elizabeth is as guilty of mistakenly judging on initial acquaintance as impetuous, romantic Marianne. When Elinor suggests that her sister has not known Willoughby long enough to know him well, Marianne's heart swells:

"You are mistaken, Elinor," said she warmly, "in supposing I know very little of Willoughby. I have not known him long indeed, but I am much better acquainted with him, than I am with any other creature in the world, except yourself and mama...Seven years would be insufficient to make some people acquainted with each other, and seven days are more than enough for others."

Marianne is once again trusting to her errant inner guide. As I have just reminded your sister heroine-in-training, Wickham's pleasing appearance also causes Lizzy to grant credibility to his story before she knows anything verifiable of his character or history: "...there was truth in his looks," she tells Jane, dismissing the latter's juster defense of Mr. Darcy. To Elizabeth, Wickham's countenance—a very handsome one, to be sure—is proof enough of his amiability and trustworthiness. And as you know, her feeling towards Mr. Darcy could with some accuracy be described as "hatred at first sight." But her sentiments and his undergo so material a change that she later says of Mr. Darcy's letter: "The feelings of the person who wrote, and the person who received it, are now so widely different from what they were then, that every unpleasant circumstance attending it, ought to be forgotten." You also know which man of the two—

the one to whom affection was freely given at the first sight of him or the one by whom it was earned—became the idol of millions—nay, hundreds of millions—of women:

If gratitude and esteem are good foundations of affection, Elizabeth's change of sentiment will be neither improbable nor faulty. But if otherwise, if the regard springing from such sources is unreasonable or unnatural, in comparison of what is so often described as arising on a first interview with its object, and even before two words have been exchanged, nothing can be said in her defence, except that she had given somewhat of a trial to the latter method, in her partiality for Wickham, and that its ill-success might perhaps authorise her to seek the other less interesting mode of attachment.

Not after one conversation but over the course of four months did Elizabeth learn enough of Darcy's character to "comprehend that he was exactly the man, who, in disposition and talents, would most suit her." And if any heroes should happen to be reading this book, I hope you have learned from Mr. Darcy's error: his first impression of Elizabeth—"tolerable; but not handsome enough to tempt [*him*]" was equally mistaken. She is without a doubt as delightful a creature as ever appeared in print.

The minds of men and women alike run too much upon the phenomenon I understand to be comprehended in the word "chemistry." The charm of personal attraction is intoxicating, but beware the dangers of an attachment formed solely or even primarily on such superficial grounds. When I was merely twenty, I fell in love with a young Irishman. We knew very little of one another—far too little, indeed, to have fallen so deeply in love. We did everything most profligate and shocking in the way of dancing and sitting down together at the local balls. And he went off and married another and all that attraction—to what did it amount? A ghostly memory, no more. Worse, a powerful vision of romance untested by time. What foolishness...As I advised my niece Fanny,

"Anything is to be preferred or endured rather than marrying without Affection...," and I am not urging you to set aside the incalculable value of that dizzying, agitating, delightful feeling when entering into a life-long attachment. Emma Watson, quite correctly, can think of no fate worse than "marry[ing] a man [she] did not like." But you must not therefore make the mistake of thinking that a feeling of powerful attraction must arise immediately upon your acquaintance with a man or it will never be felt at all. When deciding upon a single "date," it would be better to have Elizabeth Watson's more open mind regarding the generality of the male sex: "I should not like marrying a disagreable man any more than yourself,—but I do not think there *are* very many disagreable men; –I think I could like any good humoured man with a comfortable income." A mind too romantic and particular, too fixed in opinions formed from first impressions, is likely to make habitually hasty and mistaken choices, and to live to regret them. To live, perhaps, for a long time in the shadow of a memory and so miss the sunnier pleasures of life's day. There, you have driven me to metaphor—a sure sign I must pause and clear my head of all trite figures.

Believe me very truly your affectionate friend,

Jane Austen

> **JANE AUSTEN SAYS: A HEROINE DOES NOT FALL IN LOVE AT FIRST SIGHT.**

Here is the coach at last. How Cassandra's bed does rattle! Upon my word, it has traveled a full three inches across the floor. Mine has withstood the onslaught better. Indeed, I believe it has remained perfectly still.

Chapter Six
A Heroine's Guide to S-x (A Short Chapter)

*What a woman she must be! I long to see her,
and shall certainly accept your kind invitation, that I may form some idea of those bewitching powers which can do so much—
engaging at the same time and in the same
house the affections of two men who were
neither of them at liberty to bestow them—
and all this, without the charm of youth.*
       —Reginald De Courcy, *Lady Susan*

Dear Jane Austen,

I have been going out with Bill for two years. We are both in our early thirties. We live in New York City. Bill is about to lose his cheap sublet and will have to pay a fortune to rent another apartment. I have a rent-stabilized one-bedroom. I have been dying to get married to Bill. Now he is strongly hinting that he wouldn't mind moving in with me. That is my idea of heaven. Not only would it save Bill lots of money, which we could spend on other things, but he would get used to having me around and would very likely ask me to marry him (a subject he has not yet mentioned). Don't you think?

Almost Happy

~~&~~

Dear Almost Happy Heroine,

How much self-delusion there is in almost all of our plans! Have you truly read my novels? I must ask because I find it incredible, inconceivable, impossible! that you would not know my opinion on this question already. But I must remind myself that one of the cherished stories of your time is the tale of a rich man choosing to marry a toothsome, inelegant woman (evidently considered pretty by some) whose company he was by no means the only man to purchase for ready money. So, for the instruction of you and your sister heroines-in-training I shall go over the matter again.

The disgrace attached to the domestic arrangement you describe is no longer such as to cause the same harm to innocent parties it once did, and thus I make no moral judgment here. You have expressed a desire to marry Bill and marriage is indeed the state I prefer for my heroines. I speak only of what will assist you to reach that end. If, given your mature ages, he has not proposed to you after two years of intimacy, it is most unlikely the gentleman will propose marriage once you have installed yourself as mistress of a shared household, particularly if the move has been motivated—at least in part—by financial expediency. You are seeing the matter with the same "creative eye of fancy" with which Lydia Bennet imagined her trip to Brighton. And I am sorry to say that the parallel with Lydia does not end there. Lydia lived with Wickham in the sanguine expectation he would marry her ("some time or other, and it did not much signify when") but if he had not been handsomely paid off by Mr. Darcy he would not have done so, as he openly acknowledges. And indeed when the newly-married couple first visits the Bennets, we see that "Wickham's affection for Lydia, was just what Elizabeth had expected to find it; not equal to Lydia's for him." And thereafter, "His affection for her soon sunk into indifference; her's lasted a little longer." Maria Rushworth, formerly Maria Bertram of Mansfield Park, represents a more grievous case, as the lady was already married when she ran off with Henry Craw-ford "under the idea of being really loved by a man who had long ago made his indifference clear." Can it admit of doubt, dear Heroine, how much wilful delusion is necessary to such a foolish choice? And again, the story ends badly:

She was not to be prevailed on to leave Mr. Craw-ford. She hoped to marry him, and they continued together till she was obliged to be convinced that such hope was vain, and till the disappointment and wretchedness arising from the conviction, rendered her temper so bad, and her feelings for him so like hatred, as to make them for a while each other's punishment, and then induce a voluntary separation.

Permanent happiness cannot come from the indulgence of momentary passion at the expense of higher considerations, even in those cases where the question of adultery does not arise.

In both instances the women gave—and gave up—far more than they received in return. How, exactly, will Bill be induced to marry you if you grant him all connubial privileges before he makes any commitment to you? If he is to propose at all (and that is a question very much in doubt) he will almost certainly do so when he believes that the only way he will be able to secure your affections and companionship is to marry you. And do not think you will strengthen his attachment to you—or inspire the ardent love that you fear does not now exist—by saving him money. With such mercenary concerns a man's love has nothing to do. On the contrary, he will love you only if he provides for you, NOT the other way round. (I cannot let it pass unremarked that though you may pay rent worthy of Kellynch Hall, your lodgings are more likely to resemble Mrs. Smith's "noisy parlour, and a dark bed-room behind." And your idea of heaven is to share with a man this slatternly abode—though it be strewn with your petticoats and pots of Gowland's lotion and the remnants of last night's cold chicken—and this before you have truly attached the gentleman? It is by any rational view incomprehensible.) For more on this matter read on, and trade your illusion of future happiness, which is more likely in reality to resemble Maria's disappointment and wretchedness, for the real thing now.

Yours,

Jane Austen

> **JANE AUSTEN SAYS: A HEROINE SEEKING MARRIAGE DOES NOT LIVE WITH A HERO UNTIL HE IS HER HUSBAND.**

Dear Jane Austen,

I just met a guy two weeks ago after five years of celibacy. He is coming on really strong. He wants us to spend just about every night together, certainly every weekend. We've been out to dinner, to the beach, but I haven't invited him into my apartment because I think I know where that will lead. He has told me he is in love with me and I think I'm in love too. I think he's it. Tell me, Jane, how soon is too soon for love and sex?

Sex-starved and Hungry

~~&~~

Dear Hungry Heroine,

The gentleman's "coming on really strong" is no indication of the depth of his attachment to you. It may be genuine attachment or it may be false, but either way it is too soon for it to be judged the sort that will last. If you merely seek physical gratification, it matters not whether you wait or proceed. But my heroines seek the security of lasting love and marriage, so I will advise you with that end in mind. (By the bye, I never married myself, as you well know, but, fortunately for me, writers do not have to inhabit the stories they tell. I need hardly tell you that I have great powers of imagination and observation. Indeed, it is well known that we authors more often than not stand back and observe while *vous autres* act.)

I have heard shockingly ill-bred remarks suggesting that I punished with ignoble fates those of my female characters who were carried away by passion and so fell from the state of innocence desirable in a heroine. My harsh judgment is presumed by these critics to arise from my own distaste for—even my fear of!— erotic passion. Leaving aside the question of how much I felt or did not feel personally in such matters, I must beg to be acquitted on more obvious grounds. To wit: indulgence in passion unsanctioned by legal and holy bonds was almost certain to be the death of hope for any woman desiring to live out her days in respectability and comfort, blessed with connubial peace and happiness. For you do not take into ac- count the near certainty that in my day passion indulged would lead to the birth of children. The stain of illegitimacy on mother and child was great. And do you not know how dangerous a place was childbed? Indeed, the death might well be more than a figura- tive one! More than one of my poor sisters (sisters-in- law, you would be scrupulous in saying) died when bringing children into the world. Dear Edward, whom I have just left downstairs, loved his wife so much that he would drag little Fanny out of her mother's bed if he found her there when he arrived home from a journey, sending her to her own room so that he might enjoy his wife's company. Their love led to no fewer than eleven children–and the last was finally his mother's bane. Elizabeth was dead at thirty-five, very shortly after her lying-in. But it did not take ten to do the evil: Charles's twenty-four-year-old wife died giving birth to their fourth daughter, poor little crea- ture, who followed her mother very soon thereafter. To risk such danger for fleeting passion, no matter how strongly felt in the moment, would show a degree of foolishness I should never wish to see in a young woman I cared about.

I need hardly say that even if the event proved the woman strong enough to survive the physical ordeal, she would almost certainly have rendered herself unfit in the eyes of any respectable gentleman to be his wife. Unless she were very rich indeed, she was therefore dooming herself to a life of poverty as well as disgrace. Think of Colonel Brandon's Eliza, seduced, abandoned, and castigated by Marianne's darling, Willoughby. He has only contempt for the attachment to him—"the violence of her passions, the weakness of her understanding,"—that renders her vulnerable to his seduction. I am neither condoning nor condemning these laws of life, but merely showing the truth, as I always do.

But stay, it has just occurred to me.... I hesitate to betray family secrets, but if I conceal this one I shall not be entirely truthful and you would indeed be justified in suspecting me of other shifts and equivocations. In truth I have heard my father whisper things about his sister Philadelphia. I have told you the story of how she journeyed to India as a girl in search of a husband. It has been rumoured in the family that her daughter, Cousin Eliza, was not her husband's child. But if Aunt Phila did succumb to passion, and abandon herself to the embraces of her husband's dashing young partner, Warren Hastings, either her much older husband did not know or else he made his peace with the business, preferring to keep his wife and his reputation—in England, at least—and claim little Betsy as his own rather than be called a cuckold and remain forever childless. But such extraordinary arrangements, where all parties behave in a civilized and prudent manner after the fact, are so rare that they should be discounted as examples. And, after all, this was only a story heard in whispers around Steventon about events in distant Eastern reaches of the Empire. I should not be at all surprised to learn it was no truer than the tales of Scheherazade. But then, Eliza did have the most extraordinary life—as romantic as the favourite stories of any of my heroines—and why should the true history of her conception be any more in the common way? Still, it is most shocking to think one's aunt could behave in such a manner....

In your day, Hungry Heroine, things are different, I know. Women are not fated to bear children they do not want. And yet some things from my century cast their shadow into yours, and the ease with which conception is prevented has its bad side, eliminating as it does the absolute necessity of a woman's remaining chaste until marriage. For as a rule, men still do not want women of easy virtue for their wives. And they still form attachments to women in different ways, and according to a different calendar, than women use in falling in love with them. The longer you make a hero wait for intimacy, the more powerful will grow his regard for you. Not only will he learn to love you through a greater knowledge of your character, but if, like Henry Crawford, he is accustomed to winning too easily hearts (and bodies), your surprising resistance will only increase his desire.

Remember Jane Bennet's wise words to her sister, which I quoted to Misanthropic Heroine: "Women fancy admiration means more than it does." This often wilful idea of a man's intentions seems to a woman to grant her the permission to indulge his desire for physical intimacy before he has actually made his intentions known. Like Marianne, such women live in expectation only, also like Marianne, to be devastated when their hopes are shown to be false. Happy for Marianne that she did not live in your age of accelerated intimacy, for while it is hard to imagine how she could have been more strongly affected by Willoughby's perfidy, physical union strengthens a woman's bond to a man many times over, and she might well have succeeded in her attempt at self-destruction. We can blame lively young men for their lack of caution, but it would be more effective if women would take some care of their hearts rather than expecting men to behave with the circumspection they generally lack. To be sure, Henry Crawford should have stayed away from Mansfield Park when he became conscious of the effect his presence was having on the Bertram sisters, and he would have,

had he been more in the habit of examining his own motives, and of reflecting to what the indulgence of his idle vanity was tending; but, thoughtless and selfish from prosperity and bad example, he would not look beyond the present moment.

Julia and Maria are an amusement to him, and he gladly returns to Mansfield, "and was welcomed thither quite as gladly by those whom he came to trifle with farther." Men, alas, are very often thoughtless and selfish in such matters. They do not look beyond the present moment. If women would not be hurt, they must not allow themselves to be trifled with.

Far better to emulate Fanny Price who, in response to the general surprise created by her refusal of the aforementioned Henry Crawford's proposal, wisely replies,

"...surely I was not to be teaching myself to like him only because he was taking, what seemed, very idle notice of me.... How then was I to be—to be in love with him the moment he said he was with me? How was I to have an attachment at his service, as soon as it was asked for?"

Fanny is not the most admired among my heroines, but you will never hear greater wisdom from any of the others.

Or, if Fanny suits you not, be like dear Emma, proud and self-contained, believing she can do very well without a husband and keeping her boundaries firm—until, that is, she recognizes her deep love for Mr. Knightley, the knowledge striking "with the speed of an arrow." (And is not her relationship with that gentleman—rather like that of a pupil to her master, child to the powerful father Emma had not in Mr. Woodhouse—deliciously suggestive, allowing passion to build as love grows over many years?) How much more valuable is the possession of a woman like this to the man who has won her through long and faithful service!

I hear some would-be heroines whispering that once again I am suppressing my novel in letters, *Lady Susan.* Yes, she was a middle-aged adulteress, scandalously wicked, and yes, she is ten times more interesting and attractive than any other character in the novel. Did I sympathise with her in spite of myself, as many readers have suspected? She is punished for her immoral ways, and you will notice that I never make such a woman central in my work again, so I leave it to you to determine the answer. But if you can keep her hardness of heart and treat love as a game, by all means use every art and contrivance at your disposal to win hearts and break them as you please. You have my permission to do so.... You are shocked. You fear you have stumbled upon a French authoress in error. Do not blanch, Hungry Heroine: I say this knowing full well that neither you nor any other young lady reading these letters will be able to take that dare. And if you have not Lady Susan's ability to keep your heart free from attachment—as I warrant you have not—then you had better save your entire self until such time as you have a promise from your young man—or you shall soon enough be consumed by misery, and writing me, I warrant, another letter before Michaelmas.

Yours ever,

Jane Austen

> **A HEROINE DOES NOT MISTAKE FLEETING PASSION FOR TRUE LOVE AND DEVOTION.**

Ah, me. The storm howls with a melancholy voice. How sad to think of so many women in my family dying in childbed. My own children—my novels, you know—have given me as much pleasure and not so many pangs as my nieces and nephews have given their mamas. I could no more forget any one of my darlings than a mother could forget her sucking child. My blackest hours—stretching out to a full decade—came when I was unable to conceive, but for the stunted little story of The Watsons, poor neglected creature.

Who is to say where the other road might have led? If Tom had taken me back to Ireland as his wife I would have given the world little Tom Lefroy, Jenny and Cass, George and Henry—Henry, who would no doubt have been a naughty, clever child and his mother's favourite. Emma Woodhouse and Anne Elliot would never have been born. In that case I would know a little more from experience about the subject of your letter, Hungry Heroine. But then no one—except perhaps little Jenny and Cass—would ever care to know my opinion of it.

Chapter Seven
What a Heroine Should Know About Marriage

*"...I look upon the Frasers to be about as un-
happy as most other married people."*
—Mary Crawford, *Mansfield Park*

Dear Jane Austen,

My boyfriend has asked me to marry him. So what
is my problem? I want to get married and every one of
my girlfriends wants the same thing. Only—if any of
my previous boyfriends had asked me I would have
said yes to them too. Some of them came back a year
or more later and did ask, but by then I had absolutely no interest. And I am sooo glad I didn't marry
any of them, although at the time I was madly in love
and would have accepted a proposal in a heartbeat.
So how do I know it's right this time? How do I know I
won't look back in a few years and wonder how I
could have made such a bad choice? In short, how
does a heroine know which man to marry?

Affianced

~~&~~

Dear Affianced Heroine,

Your question is a good one—so good that it forms
the basis for many of my stories. For in my day, even

more than in yours, that question and its answer
would completely determine the greatest part of a
heroine's life. Observe, if you will, how many of my
heroines first wish to marry the wrong man: Elizabeth
fancies Wickham, Emma Frank Churchill, Marianne
Willoughby. Women are not alone in bestowing their
affections on the wrong person initially: gentlemen in
my novels go so far as proposing to the wrong women,
thereby becoming unfortunately entangled: James
Morland chooses Isabella Thorpe and Edward Ferrars
Lucy Steele. Edmund Bertram barely escapes marrying Mary Crawford. By publicly showing a preference
for her, Captain Wentworth finds himself almost
engaged to Louisa Musgrove without any such inten-
tion or desire on his part. These are the lucky ones,
those who learned their mistakes in time, before
irrevocably committing themselves. My novels are
also full of examples of the bad marriages that result
in that sad majority of cases where the parties do not
realize—or correct—their errors in time. To save you
from the anguish of a bad marriage, or of a divorce
(while easily obtained in your era, a most unhappy
experience nonetheless), I shall outline here what
makes for a good choice in a spouse, and what a bad.

First of all, let us consider the broken engagements
and informal attachments just mentioned. How could
these mistaken bonds be forged? Again, the answer
goes back to my discussion of the power of fancy.
Elizabeth is infatuated with Wickham's charm and
good looks, and the same can be said regarding
Marianne and Willoughby, and Emma and Frank
Churchill. (And Emma's imagination is so powerful
that her impressions of Mr. Churchill and her preference for him were formed before they even met! I
understand this is a phenomenon not infrequently
met with in your era amongst women seeking suitors
on the Internet.) Each woman attributes virtues to
the man on the strength of his superficial appeal and,
aided by her powerful imagination, spins a romantic
story about him. Only Marianne seriously suffers
from her mistake, since of the three only her relationship goes beyond flirtation. Each heroine is taken in,

and can only after living through her great moment of truth recognize her true hero—in each case a quite different man from her first favourite. I shall return to these examples at the end of my letter.

As for the mistaken men, Edmund Bertram is so entranced by Mary Crawford's beauty, wit, and accomplishment that he thoroughly mistakes her character, actually going so far as to consider her and my heroine Fanny alike. As readers invariably note, Mary truly is a winning creature, superior in every way except her morality. But like all objects of infatuation, the figure Edmund loves is not the real person but "the creature of [his] own imagination." Edmund's deception is more than understandable—after all, those same readers (who also, as I have noted, wanted Fanny to marry Henry Crawford) actually wish Edmund would have married Mary. And indeed, that is what makes *Mansfield Park* so interesting. I create an irresistible woman and then say: despite all her attractions, you must not allow yourself to be seduced by her charms—not by her wit nor her real sweetness at times: her heart is hollow. She is unprincipled and mercenary. Must I say it again? The world is full of such mixed characters—yet how rare is their appearance in novels! (No less a genius than Sir Walter Scott said I had the greatest talent he had ever met with for "describing the involvements and feelings and characters of ordinary life." I only wish he had expressed his admiration so warmly when he was reviewing my work years earlier!)

Indeed, Edmund Bertram is to some extent equally a fanciful creation of Mary Crawford's. She, no less than my Emma, is prone to wilful delusion at times. So is she able to shut out from her thoughts the certainty that Edmund will be a clergyman—an occupation appalling to her ("A clergyman is nothing")—and so is she repeatedly roused to anger and resentment when the "agreeable fancies" of her favourite as a gentleman of independent fortune rather than an active, resident, preaching parish clergyman—fancies she often indulges—are destroyed. From the begin-

ning of their acquaintance, both parties wilfully
ignore (to borrow again that useful if hackneyed
expression) "red flags" concerning their differing
values and views in order to sustain the illusions.

Lucy Steele's attachment to Edward Ferrars is a
rather more common sort of case, one that is frequently seen in my novels and in the world. Lucy is
described by Elinor—no doubt accurately despite
Elinor's bias in the matter—as "illiterate, artful, and
selfish." Yet this same girl seemed quite different
when Edward first met her: "The youthful infatuation
of nineteen would naturally blind him to every thing
but her beauty and good nature..." At twenty-four he
now sees his folly in believing Lucy a suitable partner;
he *now* has "no scruple in believing her capable of the
utmost meanness of wanton ill-nature." James Morland is also undeceived in time, discovering the in-
constancy and duplicity of Isabella Thorpe's character
before he makes the mistake of marrying her. Like
Lucy, Isabella had the superficial attractions—youth,
beauty, spirit—that ensnare young men and blind
them to the deeper knowledge of a woman's character
that comes only with time. (And I am afraid it is only
too true that—as Oscar Wilde, who clearly learned
much about dialogue, both witty and nonsensical,
from me, has it—good looks are "a snare that every
sensible man would like to be caught in.") These are
the fortunate few: far more prevalent in my novels are
the men who did not discover their errors in time, but
went on to wed the objects of their youthful infatuation. I shall now remind you of their experiences to
save you from a similar fate.

**JANE AUSTEN SAYS: TIME WILL TELL IF
INFATUATION WILL TURN INTO LASTING LOVE.**

Mr. Bennet is one of my most amusing creations,
and his wit often seduces readers into approving of
him. But his humour has a bitter edge, and that, you

know, comes from his unhappiness in his marriage. For he,

captivated by youth and beauty, and that appearance of good humour, which youth and beauty generally give, had married a woman whose weak understanding and illiberal mind, had very early in their marriage put an end to all real affection for her. Respect, esteem, and confidence, had vanished forever; and all his views of domestic happiness were overthrown.

He is perhaps thinking of himself when he makes this remark upon the realization that Wickham must have been paid off handsomely to marry his daughter Lydia: "...no man in his senses, would marry Lydia on so slight a temptation as one hundred a-year during my life, and fifty after I am gone." For Lydia takes after her mother in having no more in her favour than "youth, health, and good humour." Elizabeth, who rather resembles her father, has a similar view of her sister, wondering "how Lydia could ever have attached him" and concluding, with her father's dryness, when she realizes they are merely living together and not married, "For such an attachment as this, she might have sufficient charms..."

Sir Thomas Bertram of Mansfield Park is captured by Miss Maria Ward on the basis of nothing more than her great personal beauty, and he thus finds himself yoked for life to an indolent, weak-minded partner, who does nothing either to improve his character or increase his domestic enjoyment, outside of bearing him children in whose upbringing she has virtually no role. When Elinor Dashwood wondered at the "the strange unsuitableness which often existed between husband and wife" she was particularly thinking of the Palmers: "His temper might perhaps be a little soured by finding, like many others of his sex, that through some unaccountable bias in favour of beauty, he was the husband of a very silly woman..." This unsuitableness is sometimes no reflection of the worth of the individuals taken separately, but merely exposes an ill-conceived union:

consider the husband and wife in my unfinished
novel you know as *Sanditon*:

...Mrs. Parker was...evidently a gentle, amiable,
sweet-tempered woman, the properest wife in the
world for a man of strong understanding, but not of
capacity to supply the cooler reflection which her own
husband sometimes needed, and so entirely waiting
to be guided on every occasion, that whether he were
risking his fortune or spraining his ankle, she remained equally useless.

Often the unfortunate mismatching of husband and
wife has repercussions and ripples that reach far
beyond the pair, spreading the misfortune throughout
their circle. Such is the case with Elinor and
Marianne's brother John: "Had he married a more
amiable woman, he might have been made still more
respectable than he was:—he might even have been
made amiable himself..." As it is, he has married
someone "narrow-minded and selfish," who brings
out those same tendencies in himself, to the great
emotional and financial distress of my heroines and
their mother.

Though we are told that Charles and Mary Musgrove "might pass for a happy couple," with them too
we see the lost opportunity that comes from a union
that is not the best:

Charles Musgrove was civil and agreeable; in sense
and temper he was undoubtedly superior to his
wife...Anne could believe, with Lady Russell, that a
more equal match might have greatly improved him;
and that a woman of real understanding might have
given more consequence to his character, and more
usefulness, rationality, and elegance to his habits
and pursuits.

As it is, married to Anne's sister, he remains a gen-
ial fellow but not the superior gentleman he would
have become under the influence of his first choice—
Anne Elliot.

Pray, do not suspect me of believing that men are as a rule the losers in matrimonial affairs. No, indeed not. Women have a great deal to complain of—or would, if they had not chosen their fates with their eyes open, and under no compulsion. Lady Elliot, Anne's mother, succumbed to a "youthful infatuation" with Sir Walter's very good looks and high rank, and although she herself was not happy in her marriage, her superior character was such that she "humoured, or softened, or concealed his failings, and promoted his real respectability for seventeen years." And thus her "conceited, silly" husband won an excellent wife by means of attractions as superficial as those that seduce young men.

Emma's father, Mr. Woodhouse, is a more benign character but not a bit less silly than Sir Walter, and though his failings are of a different sort—he is kindly but dimwitted, having lived a life "without activity of mind or body"—he was no worthier of the woman he somehow managed to win as his bride. Emma's mother had Emma's talents and beauty and it is impossible for her to have been happy or satisfied with such a mate.

The mother of Fanny Price, who married a man without education or fortune in order to disoblige her family, found herself in time with a gross, vulgar, dirty, intemperate husband, ignorant of anything outside his naval profession and negligent of his family. With a temperament resembling that of her sister, Lady Bertam—which is to say easy and indolent, with no talent and no conversation—she would have been elevated at least to respectability and happiness by marriage to a better man. With these two at the head of the family, however, the Price household is a veritable nightmare of chaos and degradation, as poor Fanny witnesses only too closely. And yet, you know, Mr. Price is not entirely to blame. He too has a right to complain. The drastic improvement in his manners upon his making the acquaintance of his daughter's friend—an "instinctive compliment to the good manners of Mr. Crawford" shows that Mr. Price's grossness and vulgarity are not an essential part of his nature, and that a better wife would have done far more to cultivate his natural abilities and polish his rough edges.

Sometimes marriage contracts are drawn up with without any youthful infatuation to excuse a decided absence of real love between the parties. Maria Bertram, driven by a desire for wealth and independence, chooses an engagement to the inferior, stupid Mr. Rushworth, and declines to avail herself of opportunities to withdraw from the arrangement even after she falls in love with another man. In her disappointed pride, she marries Rushworth, who is quite aware of her indifference towards him and her devotion to another, and so is fully complicit in his own disastrously unhappy and brief marriage. Nor can anyone can say that Elizabeth Bennet's friend Charlotte Lucas was sadly taken in when she chose a life with the odious, unlovable Mr. Collins, though the choice deeply shocked and disgusted Elizabeth. (Women in your era are not so sadly bereft of alternatives as they were in the past, you know. They are quite capable of establishing their own households, if it comes to that.)

And now, to return to the foolish first choices of my heroines mentioned above: Marianne trades in Willoughby for the steady, faithful Colonel Brandon. She is, rather, forced into giving him up when he cruelly spurns her and makes a mercenary engagement to another. We have already discussed his sterling character, shown in his seduction and betrayal of Eliza and his jilting of Marianne. He speaks ill of both the abandoned girl and his new bride, blaming the latter for his decision to reject Marianne—even going so far as to blame her for the appalling language of his rejection. As Elinor tells her sister, his own enjoyment and ease—and never *their* happiness—ruled his behaviour with all of these women. Had Marianne married him, the marriage, with no money to supply that enjoyment and ease, would have been a misery. Marianne is doubly fortunate in escaping that fate.

Not only is her second choice, Colonel Brandon, an honorable and good man more truly attached to her, but he does not bring out Marianne's faults of incivility, selfishness, and an inclination to romantic excess the way Willoughby did. All the good marriages in my novels are to the advantage of both husband and wife, for each party brings out the best in the other, and helps overcome the deficiencies.

> **JANE AUSTEN SAYS: IN A GOOD MARRIAGE, HUSBAND AND WIFE BRING OUT THE BEST IN EACH OTHER.**

When Mr. Bennet learns of Lizzy's interest in marrying Mr. Darcy he, believing she dislikes the gentleman, tells her: "...I know that you could be neither happy nor respectable, unless you truly esteemed your husband...let me not have the grief of seeing *you* unable to respect your partner in life." Had his favourite daughter done as he did, and actually married the object of her mere infatuation, Wickham, he would be worrying with just cause. Before choosing the newly moneyed Mary King over Elizabeth, and when that scheme collapsed eloping with Lydia, Wickham had tried to marry, in secret and also for money, the fifteen-year-old Georgiana Darcy. His character is thereby shown to be, like Willoughby's, ruled by selfishness. Elizabeth was saved from that dreadful error, and went on to discover that Mr. Darcy, who struck her at first as "the last man in the world whom [she] could ever be prevailed on to marry," was in fact "exactly the man, who, in disposition and talents, would most suit her." (I must quote the lines again, for they are that important.) Elizabeth and Darcy are well suited because, Affianced Heroine, they are a perfect complement:

It was an union that must have been to the advantage of both; by her ease and liveliness, his mind might have been softened, his manners improved, and from his judgment, information, and knowledge of the world, she must have received benefit of greater importance.

Wickham, on the other hand, did nothing to foster the improvement of Elizabeth's character—indeed, he encouraged her worst tendencies—and was himself beyond improvement.

As I have just reminded you, Emma Woodhouse is infatuated with the idea of Frank Churchill even before she meets him, but the man truly suited for her could not be more different from her first favourite. What Mr. Knightley has in common with all the good husbands-to-be in my novels is the desire and the will to do all in his power for the benefit of the woman he loves. Thus, he cannot see her acting wrong without a remonstrance because as much as she will dislike his scolding, he knows it is in her best interest. After he chastises her for her cruel thoughtlessness in mocking poor, silly Miss Bates to her face on Box Hill, he says:

"This is not pleasant to you, Emma—and it is very far from pleasant to me; but I must, I will,—I will tell you truths while I can, satisfied with proving myself your friend by very faithful counsel..."

Frank Churchill, on the other hand, encourages Emma's tendency to overlook any danger to the feelings of others—in particular Jane Fairfax—when she is in a mischievous, spirited mood and they are being playful together. In openly, outrageously flirting with Emma, in making sly risky references, he is committing the double sin of bringing out Emma's thoughtless and distressing his fiancée, Jane, entirely for his own amusement. In contrast to such carelessness, when Emma does not stand to benefit from being reminded of her failures, Mr. Knightley will shield her from any painful consciousness of them. Thus, when Emma knows he is reading that part of Frank Churchill's letter that refers to the Box-Hill party, "...excepting one momentary glance at her, instantly withdrawn, in the fear of giving pain—no remembrance of Box-Hill seemed to exist." How different from the self-centered behaviour of any of the objects our heroines' mere infatuation! (And with an equal delicacy that shows them deserving of each other, Emma can no more bear to give Mr. Knightley pain, and thus, as we have seen, encourages him as a friend to speak to her of what she believes to be his love for Harriet: "...cost her what it would, she would listen.")

I have previously recounted to one of your sister heroines how Colonel Brandon, Mr. Darcy, Henry Tilney, and other heroes take pride and pleasure in serving their heroines with a love that is strong and tender, delicate and manly. But this further element of mutual improvement is not to be overlooked as a great benefit of choosing a spouse wisely. The lack of this element, as my novels show, is the primary fault of many marriages. Mr. John Knightley, married to Emma's sister Isabella,

> *was not an ill-tempered man, nor so often unreasonably cross so as to deserve such a reproach; but his temper was not his great perfection; and, indeed, with such a worshipping wife, it was hardly possible that any natural defects in it should not be increased. The extreme sweetness of her temper must hurt his.*

Each partner would have become better if married to a different type. Mr. Knightley tells Emma that "Men of sense...do not want silly wives," yet the sturdy, sensible young farmer Robert Martin does want Harriet Smith, and she is undeniably rather silly. But he is just the man to value her good qualities, sweetness and artlessness, and with his devotion, good sense, and good principles, no doubt transform whatever of silliness can be transformed into steadiness. Even Mr. Knightley describes her as "infinitely to be preferred by any man of sense and taste to such a woman as Mrs. Elton." Emma is right in thinking also that "Harriet would have been a better match" and that the society of his chosen bride would do Mr. Elton no good, encouraging his tendency towards meanness and self-importance. And

yet...my refusal to write stories that meet the definition of fiction given by that same clever Irishman—
"The good ended happily, and the bad unhappily"—
compels me in honesty to admit that some men are
not merely insensible of the shame or the danger of
having chosen badly; they positively delight in their
inferior helpmates. Mr. Elton is thoroughly pleased
with his bride, despite her being, in Emma's words,
"self-important, presuming, familiar, ignorant, and ill-
bred." And John Dashwood is all admiration for his
wife, trusting her judgment and following her advice,
though she is mean-spirited, grasping, selfish, and
rude. But no right-thinking man could be happy with
such a wife, or fail to recognize and regret his own
lost opportunity to become a better man. Frank
Churchill, on the other hand, *has* chosen better for
himself, and as Mr. Knightley says, "...his character
will improve, and acquire from her's the steadiness
and delicacy of principle that it wants." I dare say
Jane will also benefit from the match: her seriousness
and reserve will be tempered by exposure to Frank's
high spirits and playfulness.

Fanny rightly believes that Mary Crawford does not
deserve Edmund, judging as she does that if his
influence in this "season of love" has not yet improved
her character it never will. But as I wrote, Miss Crawford partakes of "the general nature of women, which
would lead her to adopt the opinions of the man she
loved and respected, as her own." Had they in the end
married, Mary Crawford would have been made better
by Edmund, and no doubt my entire family would
have cheered her on in bringing more ease to his
character, which has been criticised as being rather
stiff and serious. After all, a greater disparity exists
between the high-spirited Louisa Musgrove and the
sensitive, poetry-loving Captain Benwick, yet, as
Anne Elliot believes of their future union, "...they
would soon grow more alike. He would gain cheerful-
ness, and she would learn to be an enthusiast for
Scott and Lord Byron...." Indeed, I would not venture
to say this in Fanny Price's hearing, but she and
Henry Crawford might both have gained if his suit to

win her had been successful. Even putting its particular application to one side, we may learn wisdom
from Edmund's advice to Fanny on the union of their
opposing natures:

"Your being so far unlike, Fanny, does not in the
smallest degree make against the probability of your
happiness together...I am myself convinced that it is
rather a favourable circumstance. I am perfectly
persuaded that the tempers had better be unlike; I
mean unlike in the flow of the spirits, in the manners,
in the inclination for much or little company, in the
propensity to talk, or to be silent, to be grave or to be
gay."

The fact that this is a useful position for Edmund to
hold, since he and Mary Crawford are so unlike in
temper, does not make it any less a valid one, as the
example of Elizabeth and Darcy shows.

My own parents had a rather good partnership, you
know, working together to run the boys' school when
I was young and in later years, before the passing of
my dear father, enjoying their time in Bath as rather
a holiday. (I confess I have trouble comprehending
the joy they took in the parade and silliness of that
place—especially with the memory of the beautiful
countryside around Steventon to stand as a contrast—but it is indeed true that one half of the world
cannot understand the pleasures of the other.) For in
addition to the excitement of romantic attachment,
the natural ability to work together as partners is an
important element in a successful marriage. We see
more than once how well Emma and Mr. Knightley
work in concert, usually in an attempt to prevent Mr.
Woodhouse from either experiencing or causing
agitation. In one scene Mr. Woodhouse's criticism of
the way the affairs of his daughter's family are han-
dled causes his son-in-law—quite understandably, I
believe—to respond harshly to the perceived attack.
Emma and Mr. Knightley are united in their efforts to
head off any unpleasantness with various diversions.
In another, Mr. Woodhouse's extreme nervousness
about the snowy condition of the roads on a night

when there is a small party at Randalls prompts the company to put forth their different opinions about what should be done, which of course only makes him more nervous. And then:

Mr. Knightley and Emma settled it in a few brief sentences: thus—

"Your father will not be easy; why do not you go?"

"I am ready, if the others are."

"Shall I ring the bell?"

"Yes, do."

They work together smoothly, as husband and wife will be called on to do innumerable times over the course of a marriage.

Although the nature of the crisis in *Persuasion* is more serious, notice the similarity in the way Frederick Wentworth confers with Anne Elliot concerning the question of how to inform Louisa's parents of her serious accident in the least distressing way, which he believes means not allowing her distraught sister Henrietta to do it:

"I have been considering what we had best do. She must not appear at first. She could not stand it. I have been thinking whether you had not better remain in the carriage with her, while I go in and break it to Mr. and Mrs. Musgrove. Do you think this a good plan?"

She did: he was satisfied, and said no more.

Anne takes pleasure in this display of his "deference for her judgment," an honor he paid her also when he looked to her for guidance in the moments just after the accident, and then followed her instructions without question. What a comfort for a man to have a wife like that, and not a silly, useless creature, however amiable or pretty—and, as Anne is those as well, he loses nothing. Even Henry Crawford admires Fanny's understanding and manners, and furthermore, he "had too much sense not to feel the worth of good principles in a wife..." A man would be lucky indeed to esteem the judgment of a woman he married under the influence of infatuation, without a true understanding of her character. That is not to say it does not happen—as my books also show—but that it is leaving a great deal to chance. In time these couples will be as well versed in each other's thoughts as are Captain Harville and his wife, who no longer even have a need for speech in order to come to agreement in times of crisis: "a look between him and his wife decided what was to be done."

Perhaps my favorite married couple in all my writing is Admiral and Mrs. Croft. Anne too thinks they present "a most attractive picture of happiness" in married life as they stroll the streets of Bath together. And yet, to be sure, they did come to an understanding very quickly. The way the couple collaborates in steering the Admiral's gig, Mrs. Croft giving the reins a tug or putting out her hand when necessary, strikes Anne as "no bad representation of the general guidance of their affairs"—a most attractive picture indeed!

Anne Elliot, Catherine Morland, Fanny Price—these of my heroines end up with their first loves; for them there is no need for a mistaken first choice and subsequent correction. But time was necessary for them to know that the choice was the correct one. Even Anne and Captain Wentworth entered married life with a much deeper knowledge of each other than they had during their first engagement: "more tender, more tried, more fixed in a knowledge of each other's character, truth, and attachment; more equal to act, more justified in acting."

Passion and infatuation are not the proper foundations for marriage, though the kind of entertainment preferred by women fosters the illusion that they are. Only those parts of passion that cause your higher, more generous self to flourish are to play a part in your decision; only those parts of infatuation that will not fade over time should have a voice in the debate. My observation tells me that you twenty-first-century heroines, with far fewer restrictions on choosing a husband than the women of my day had, are not making decisions that bid any fairer for happiness. So, consider: if your fiancé is more Mr. Knightley than Frank Churchill, you are choosing wisely and have my blessing.

Yours very sincerely,

Jane Austen

~~&~~

Dear Jane Austen,

I don't think I want to get married. I don't see any happy marriages. Does a heroine have to end up married?

Satisfied Single

~~&~~

Dear Single Heroine,

As none of my heroines remain single, I suppose I shall have to speak from my own experience. The great Dr. Johnson is one of my favorite authors, you know, but I must disagree with his celebrated maxim that "Marriage has many pains but celibacy has no pleasures." That is to say, having witnessed the marriages of all my brothers—for they all married, you know—I can attest to the truth of the first part. It is only the second part that I dispute.

What, are you back to visit me again, Cass? Is not this true? Yes, you are quite right. I do not often think of George, poor fellow.

I have not spoken accurately, Single Heroine. We do have a brother who never married, but he has lived since he was a child with a very good family. They watch him—for he cannot take care of himself. It is so very sad. My parents' firstborn, named for my father. One of the great pains—indeed, the greatest—of my parents' marriage, I am quite certain. I do not wish to dwell on the subject....

What say you, Cass, is it your view that celibacy can boast any pleasures that would make it a formidable rival of matrimony?

My sister frowns and tells me she must hasten away again. She insists I leave off writing and come down to dinner at once. She is very reserved. Ah, my readers, I fear Cass has not found much pleasure in life since her fiancé Tom died all those years ago, and all her plans for a home of her own and children died with him. You see, she has not had the joy I have had in my children, each one a hold upon happiness. Her joy has been all through me, and that is not the same at all. I have not lacked for pleasure while I have had *them* to occupy my time.

No doubt Cass can inform you better than I can what wayward tendencies in my character would have been improved by the right husband. The question of marriage did arise more than once in my life, you know. I have told you about Tom Lefroy, and Harris Bigg-Wither. But I don't believe I've told you about the other gentleman, the one Cass and I met that summer in Devonshire. I always loved the sea on those fine sunshiny days! I would bathe until I was quite exhausted. You do not ever picture me descending the steps of a bathing machine and plunging into the chilly waves, I dare say. Yes, that young man was a something between Tom, the object of my youthful infatuation who could not marry me, and Harris, whom I would not marry though he had everything in his favour except the possession of my heart. I can see the young man now. We were to meet again the following summer, on the coast, near the glorious, sparkling sea. And then, suddenly, we got news that he had died. And then, I knew there would be no more occasions to think of my marrying, though I was still quite young enough to have had my share of lying in.

I hope I have answered your question, Single Heroine. I don't believe I have any more to say on the matter right now.

Yours,

Jane Austen

Chapter Eight
Beauty Tips for Heroines

...I was very well pleased—particularly (pray tell Fanny) with a small portrait of Mrs. Bingley, excessively like her...Mrs. Bingley is exactly herself, size, shaped face, features & sweetness; there never was a greater likeness. She is dressed in a white gown, with green ornaments, which convinces me of what I had always supposed, that green was a favourite colour with her. I dare say Mrs. D. will be in Yellow.
—letter to Cassandra, May 24, 1813

Dear Jane Austen,

I am just average-looking and I live in a city where women outnumber men three to one. The competition is fierce! And if these women aren't perfect by nature they have the time and money to buy great beauty. They spend fortunes not only on their clothes and hair, but on something you don't know about, plastic surgery. I mean, they get new noses and breasts—they totally resculpt their bodies! Tell me, Miss Austen, what hope is their for an average gal?

Plain Jane

~~&~~

Dear Plain Heroine,

I shall try not to read any insult into your signature because I am quite sure you meant no reflection on me but were merely falling back on a commonplace phrase. While the Janes in my novels were elegant, lovely creatures—Jane Bennet and Jane Fairfax come to mind—I confess that my own appearance was more along the lines of what was to be found in real life than in romance. Cousin Phila told Eliza that I was not at all pretty at twelve years old, but I believe my appearances, like Catherine Morland's, were mending by the time I began attending the local balls—and I was certainly pretty enough to capture the heart of Tom Lefroy. Well, we need not speak of him again. A girl of twenty, flirting and dancing with her young man, must be a sad figure indeed not to strike her neighbors as rather pretty!

Do not tell Cass, but her sketch of me has given the world quite the wrong idea of my looks. No one in the family ever thought it either a good likeness or a flattering improvement on the original (as was Emma's portrait of Harriet)—but how was I to know it would be the only portrait of me to survive? No, I was never conventionally pretty and yet those who knew me found my face quite attractive. I had a natural liveliness that brought colour into my cheeks, and my eyes sparkled with merriment more often than not. I believe my tall, thin figure—I was a pretty height—would quite fit your era's fashion. When I was not in a gay mood, I suppose I did not look so well—somewhat forbidding, perhaps—but as you shall see, that can be said of us all. (I speak of myself only as I was, for no one much cares what a spinster over the age of forty looks like—although I understand women of my age are considered still rather young in your era. Every age has its improvements.)

And now, to your question. Has it escaped your notice that my heroines are not as a rule the most beautiful women in my novels? Emma is perhaps the only one not surpassed by another in the aspect of looks and she, as Mr. Knightley says, is not "person-

ally vain" and is "little occupied with [her beauty]."
Jane Bennet is better-looking than her sister Elizabeth, yet there is no doubt which is the superior
creature—which is to say, the heroine. For all her
loveliness of face and character, Jane has not Elizabeth's liveliness and wit—and it is moreover Jane's
good sense and sweetness that ensure her face will
continue to please as years pass. While we are with
the Bennets, allow me to point out that whereas Mary
is the only plain one of the family, her unattractive-
ness cannot be attributed to her unfortunate looks,
but rather to her boring, pedantic, humourless, vain
character. Grace and manner are essential to any
heroine over the age of seventeen, before which some
awkwardness is perhaps to be excused for a short
time longer.

With the exception of Jane Bennet, those girls
whose beauty surpasses that of my heroines are
invariably so flawed in other ways as to make them
incapable, despite their beauty, of achieving their
ends. Elizabeth Elliot is a great enough beauty, even
at twenty-nine, to suit her father's exacting judgment,
yet even when very young she failed to win the heart
of the man she preferred. Indeed, she remains un-
married at the novel's end. Her manner is so unattractive—vacant, snobbish, and cold—that even her
beauty cannot overcome it.

In *Mansfield Park*, neither Maria Bertram nor Mary
Crawford, both beautiful women, succeeds in ultimately winning the man she loves. Their beauty and
other charms take them a good part of the way, but
cannot be counted on to bring them across the finish
line when combined with such serious character
flaws as these women possess. The same can be said
for Catherine Morland's "dear friend" Isabella Thorpe,
whose beauty wins her the attention of many men,
but whose shallowness and vanity lose her that
attention almost as quickly. In your own world, Plain
Heroine, surely you see the same progression: beautiful women have an easier time capturing attention,
but if good looks are the extent of what they bring to

an attachment, they will not be able to hold that attention for long. (And by the bye, have you never noticed how often—in real life—men leave beautiful women for plainer ones?) I reminded your sister, Affianced Heroine, of the miserable marriages that resulted when men chose wives purely on the basis of personal beauty. As I have said, Lady Bertram, Mrs. Bennet, and Mrs. Palmer were beauties, and with that attraction alone won their unfortunate husbands. The ease with which divorce is obtained and excused in your era ensures that the husbands of empty-headed beauties will not be equally ready to settle into their disappointment for life. (As I have noted before, good looks in men can be equally deceiving. While heroes should be handsome if they possibly can be, the good looks of Sir Walter Elliot, Willoughby, and Wickham are a handsome screen covering very bad characters.)

Marianne is more beautiful than her sister Elinor, yet she is a good illustration of the truth I referred to earlier, that beauty is very closely tied to the spirit. When Marianne is despondent over Willoughby's desertion, she becomes "careless of her appearance" in a way that draws notice to her condition. As her thoughtless brother remarks,

"...there is something very trying to a young woman who *has been* a beauty, in the loss of her personal attractions. You would not think it perhaps, but Marianne *was* remarkably handsome a few months ago; quite as handsome as Elinor.—Now you see it is all gone."

The anguish in her soul destroys, temporarily, her great beauty. As one whose own comeliness fluctuated with my state of mind—whether joyful or melancholy, anxious or calm—I can attest that the inner life contributes a great deal, for better or worse, to one's outward appearance.

Anne Elliot "had been a very pretty girl, but her bloom had vanished early," so that when Frederick Wentworth sees her years later he thinks her "wretchedly altered." But Anne has been deeply un-happy for years, full of regret for her decision to break her engagement with him, and when she is happy again, secure in the knowledge that he continues to love her, her beauty returns. How many things be-sides physical appearance contribute to the percep-tion of a woman's beauty! For on the trip to the sea-side resort of Lyme—even before she knows of his feelings—Anne's bloom is "restored by the fine wind which had been blowing on her complexion, and by the animation of eye which it had also produced." When another gentleman, noticing her appearance, looks at Anne with admiration, Captain Wentworth is roused to look at her again himself, and to perceive her differently as well. Men do not always judge women's beauty by purely objective standards, which is a useful thing for both pretty girls and plain ones to know.

Henry Crawford is deeply struck by Fanny's rapt appearance while she listens to her beloved brother William: "Fanny's attractions increased—increased two-fold—for the sensibility which beautified her complexion and illumined her countenance, was an attraction in itself." Margaret Watson's appearance, in contrast, is diminished by her manner: "the sharp and anxious expression of her face made her beauty in general little felt." And time alone makes altera-tions in our judgments of the looks of those with whom we are becoming acquainted, whether male or female. Henry Crawford himself will serve to illustrate my point nicely:

> *Her brother was not handsome; no, when they first saw him, he was absolutely plain, black and plain.... The second meeting proved him not so very plain; he was plain, to be sure, but then he had so much coun-tenance, and his teeth were so good, and he was so well made, that one soon forgot he was plain; and, after a third interview...he was no longer allowed to be called so by any body. He was, in fact, the most agreeable young man the sisters had ever known....*

Henry Crawford's appearance does not change, but the perception of it changes as he becomes better known to the Bertrams. Elinor makes this point with regard to Edward Ferrars:

"His abilities in every respect improve as much upon acquaintance as his manners and person. At first sight, his address is certainly not striking; and his person can hardly be called handsome, till the expression of his eyes, which are uncommonly good, and the general sweetness of his countenance, is perceived. At present, I know him so well, that I think him really handsome; or, at least, almost so."

Why, even Elizabeth Bennet only strikes Mr. Darcy at first as merely "tolerable":

Mr. Darcy had at first scarcely allowed her to be pretty; he had looked at her without admiration at the ball; and when they next met, he looked at her only to criticise. But no sooner had he made it clear to himself and his friends that she had hardly a good feature in her face, than he began to find it was rendered uncommonly intelligent by the beautiful expression of her dark eyes.

And it is not long before he considers her "one of the handsomest women of [his] acquaintance." Clearly, it is not Elizabeth's looks that have bewitched him. A woman becomes more beautiful to a man as he becomes more attracted to her other qualities, just as the attraction of a beauty diminishes if her behaviour fails to live up to the promise of her face.

Elizabeth Bennet is certainly pretty by any objective standards, so perhaps a more extreme example is called for. Elizabeth Elliot does not believe her friend Mrs. Clay, without the least personal attraction to recommend her, can be any threat to the status of Sir Walter as a single man—he being the harshest judge of appearance imaginable, who has frequently remarked upon her physical flaws. But the wiser Anne knows otherwise:

"There is hardly any personal defect," replied Anne, which an agreeable manner might not gradually reconcile one to."

"I think very differently," answered Elizabeth, shortly; "an agreeable manner may set off handsome features, but can never alter plain ones."

Ah, Plain Heroine—you know which of the sisters has been given the correct opinion in this matter. Except, perhaps, in the most extreme cases, it matters little whether someone is objectively good-looking or ill-looking if there is time enough for a knowledge of other characteristics to grow; initial impressions based on appearance can be reversed in either direction. And so, only the most foolish characters in my novels are vain about their own looks or overly concerned with the personal appearance of others. The slow-witted, indolent Lady Bertram respects only beauty and wealth, and the same might be said of the vain, small-minded Sir Walter. And are there indeed any sillier creatures in all my works?

In conclusion, Plain Heroine, do your best with your appearance but pay more attention to cultivating your inner beauty using the knowledge gained from these letters and your hero will find you as bewitching as Mr. Darcy found Elizabeth Bennet.

Your faithful friend,

Jane Austen

JANE AUSTEN SAYS: A HEROINE'S BEAUTY IS MORE A MATTER OF HER CHARACTER AND MANNER THAN HER PHYSICAL FEATURES.

Dear Jane Austen,

I am, I admit, kind of obsessed with clothes. I don't make much money but I spend a lot on designer clothes—that's very expensive stuff. What do you think about my obsession? Should a heroine be so focused on what she puts on her back?

Stylish

~~&~~

Dear Stylish Heroine,

I shall not scold you too harshly because I do not know enough about your passion to determine the extent of its influence on your life. You would be a strange female indeed if you did not care at all about your appearance, or believe that you would turn the head of a hero with a new bonnet or gown. But if we examine my novels, we shall see that those women who share your great interest in clothing and speak of it to others believing it is of as much interest to *them* are never my heroines.

To be sure, seventeen-year-old Catherine Morland, on the eve of the cotillion ball, may be forgiven for dwelling on the subject. The passage is rather long, but I still find it quite charming and therefore I beg your indulgence while I quote it at some length:

What gown and what head-dress she should wear on the occasion became her chief concern...she lay awake ten minutes on Wednesday night debating between her spotted and her tamboured muslin, and nothing but the shortness of the time prevented her buying a new one for the evening.... It would be mortifying to the feelings of many ladies, could they be made to understand how little the heart of man is affected by what is costly or new in their attire; how little it is biassed by the texture of their muslin, and how unsusceptible of peculiar tenderness towards the spotted, the sprigged, the mull or the jackonet. Woman is fine for her own satisfaction alone. No man will admire her the more, no woman will like her the better for it.

"Neatness and fashion" are enough for men and, I confess, so they have always been enough for me. All my ambition that way was to be tidy and to avoid as much as possible the torment of hairdressing. Cassandra, for her part, rather enjoyed the minute details of our own new muslins and bonnets and she forced me on pain of death to describe them to her in my letters. But the latest fashions from London have never held interest for me and I hated to write about them. Such unnatural styles, with bosoms forced up by stays—and the hats!—upon my word, it would be more natural to have flowers growing out of ladies' heads than fruit! You can be sure when anyone in my novels speaks of such matters I am amusing myself with their foolishness.

Mrs. Allen thinks and speaks of nothing but clothing. Her own attire interests her the most but she notices and remembers nothing about other people besides their clothing and jewelry. In response to Catherine's desperate insistence that Mrs. Allen must know someone in Bath as they sit down amongst strangers in the tea-room, she says,

"I don't upon my word—I wish I did. I wish I had a large acquaintance here with all my heart, and then I should get you a partner.—I should be so glad to have you dance. There goes a strange-looking woman! What an odd gown she has got on!—How old-fashioned it is! Look at the back."

Mrs. Allen only comes to life when she speak of this trivial subject.

Her passionate engagement is shown in her breaking off her placid nonsense to exclaim over the details of dress. Have I yet demonstrated to you that such a mania for fashion is unbecoming? Perhaps you need another example. I do believe Mrs. Allen to be one of my finest comic creations, and therefore I gladly supply you with some additional dialogue of hers, this time in an exchange with Henry Tilney:

"My dear Catherine," said she, "do take this pin out of my sleeve; I am afraid it has torn a hole already; I shall be quite sorry if it has, for this is a favourite gown, though it cost but nine shillings a yard."

"That is exactly what I should have guessed it, madam," said Mr. Tilney, looking at the muslin.

"Do you understand muslins, sir?"

"Particularly well..."

"And pray, sir, what do you think of Miss Morland's gown?"

"It is very pretty, madam," said he, gravely examining it; "but I do not think it will wash well; I am afraid it will fray."

What a shame this novel will not find an audience before I... Was I ever more delighted with my own brilliant nonsense? I do wish I could have the pleasure of hearing what Henry and Cass and my rather silly neighbors have to say about it.... But forgive me. I stray from the subject at hand.

Mrs. Bennet also has a mind empty enough of matters of substance to allow room for a professed interest in the question of long sleeves. And while the whole family is in a state of extreme distress and anxiety over Lydia's disappearance with Wickham, Mrs. Bennet is concerned about her daughter's wedding clothes—when there is as yet no reason to think there will even be a wedding! When Mr. Bennet later refuses to advance money to buy those same wedding clothes, "She was more alive to the disgrace, which the want of new clothes must reflect on her daughter's nuptials, than to any sense of shame at her eloping and living with Wickham, a fortnight before they took place." Lydia, ever her mother's daughter, is shown talking and writing of new bonnets, gowns, and parasols, and is made "quite wild" by goods for sale in Brighton. She is the only one of the girls (except Kitty, who follows Lydia's lead in all things and therefore does not count) to whom I attribute an interest in such matters, so you may deduce from that fact my opinion of a rage for finery. (Not coincidentally, in London, the eye of silly Mrs. Palmer is "caught by every thing pretty, expensive, or new" and she is "wild to buy all.")

Although I do not emphasize it over-much, vanity about her dress is also part of Isabella Thorpe's character. While Catherine Morland may be kept awake thinking about what she will wear on the morrow, what distinguishes her from these others is that she does not speak of such tedious and vain concerns aloud. Emma Watson only speaks to her sister-in-law of her gown to take her mind off a quarrel with her husband, and Mrs. Robert Watson, who raised the subject of her dress minutes earlier, takes the bait and returns to it with pleasure:

"Do you like it?"—said she.—"I am very happy.—It has been excessively admired;—but I sometimes think the pattern too large.—I shall wear one tomorrow that I think you will prefer to this.—Have you seen the one I gave Margaret?"

Again, Stylish Heroine, to make such a fuss over one's gown, and to believe that others are interested in its pattern, is not a heroine-like way to behave. Vulgar Mrs. Elton, both bragging and fishing for compliments, continually talks of her gown, her jewelry, her hair. What is meant to be an insulting dismissal of Emma's wedding clothes—"Very little white satin, very few lace veils; a most pitiful business!" is instead but one more illustration of the absurdity of such concerns and the superiority of those with quiet good taste both in their clothes and their conversation. And I need not tell you what I think of the men in my novels who show an excessive interest in fashion. The foppish Robert Ferrars in *Sense and Sensibility* is duly mocked for displaying "the delicacy of his taste"—that is to say, his puppyism—by spending an eternity choosing a toothpick-case in a shop while he keeps Elinor and Marianne waiting to be served in turn. And what could make Lord Osborne sound sillier than his advice to Emma Watson: "You should wear half-boots.... Nothing sets off a neat ankle more than a half-boot; nankin galoshed with black looks very well.—Do not you like half-boots?" If you do not see my point, just try to imagine Mr. Knightley or Mr. Darcy saying such things!

Cass was a true beauty in her youth, as I was not, but I suppose we both became middle-aged in our appearance rather early in life. We certainly have never worn nankin boots for walking in dirty country lanes. Pattens are not fashionable, but they are certainly more practical. And after all, good health and exercise are the greatest enhancers of physical beauty. Crossness and sickliness, indolence and fretfulness—all destroy beauty, and exercise will often raise the spirits and do away with them. Emma Woodhouse has beautiful features, to be sure, but Mrs. Weston's description of her as "the complete picture of grown-up health," with "health not merely in her bloom, but in her air, her head, her glance" says more about my idea of a heroine's beauty. So do not wear your fashionable Manolo Blahniks if they will put a frown on your face and prevent you from enjoying a walk in the sweet, fresh, clear country air. And as for the beauty from within I have been recommending, I suggest that you read again the letters in the first chapter, "A Heroine's Character," if you desire to cultivate it.

I shall conclude with my darling Lizzy, who in a single scene perfectly exemplifies all that I have been urging. She has come to Netherfield, as you will recall, out of concern for her sister Jane, who has fallen ill with a cold and is staying there. While she is attending to Jane, the Bingley sisters take the opportunity to abuse her:

"She has nothing, in short, to recommend her, but being an excellent walker. I shall never forget her appearance this morning. She really looked almost wild."

"She did indeed, Louisa. I could hardly keep my countenance. Very nonsensical to come at all! Why must *she* be scampering about the country, because her sister had a cold? Her hair so untidy, so blowsy!"

Yes, and her petticoat; I hope you saw her petticoat, six inches deep in mud, I am absolutely certain; and the gown which had been let down to hide it, not doing its office."

(Would-be heroines will incidentally take note of how unattractive such jealous, mean-spirited attacks on another woman sound.) Now Miss Bingley and Mrs. Hurst are no doubt strictly correct in their catalogue of Elizabeth's sins against fashion. They are aligned with the foolish Mrs. Bennet, who warned Elizabeth she would not be fit to be seen after such a walk, to which her daughter replied, "I shall be very fit to see Jane—which is all I want." But notice the response of their brother to her purportedly objectionable appearance, and her indifference to it:

"Your picture may be very exact, Louisa," said Bingley; "but this was all lost upon me. I thought Miss Elizabeth Bennet looked remarkably well, when she came into the room this morning. Her dirty petticoat quite escaped my notice."

He also protests that her walking alone several miles through the mud "shows an affection for her sister that is very pleasing." (It is little wonder that Elizabeth looks well when she has been "jumping over stiles and springing over puddles" in the healthy, fearless, vigorous way I approve as an aid to a heroine's beauty both inner and outer.) Not only is the easygoing Bingley charmed rather than repelled by Lizzy's "indifference to decorum"; the much more fastidious Mr. Darcy is impressed in spite of himself:

"I am afraid, Mr. Darcy," observed Miss Bingley, in a half whisper, "that this adventure has rather affected your admiration of her fine eyes."

"Not at all," he replied; "they were brightened by the exercise."

With no concern at all for the impression she is making, her appearance, or the unconventionality of her behaviour, she bewitches Mr Darcy entirely. I am not recommending Elizabeth's attitude and behaviour here because they succeed with the gentlemen; rather, the gentlemen in this case are responding correctly to the correct attitude and behaviour. They are properly attractive and the men are inevitably attracted.

I am also far from recommending dirty petticoats and blowsy hair as enhancements to a woman's appearance, but just as excessive solicitude about dress often destroys its aim, so too a lack of self-consciousness about one's appearance is often the very best aid to a heroine's beauty.

Believe me ever your faithful friend,

Jane Austen

How tired I feel after my visit downstairs. I should not lie awake for long if I closed my eyes now, but I must press on for the sake of my heroines-in-training. I am afraid no one could call me the picture of health today. Upon my word, I am as querulous as Mary Musgrove, as fretful as Kitty Bennet, as nervous as Isabella Knightley. But this mood will never answer. With so many sad and anxious letters still to be read I must defer self-pity for a while longer.

Chapter Nine
Should a Heroine Care About Money?

> *...[T]hey were neither of them quite enough in love to think that three hundred and fifty pounds a-year would supply them with the comforts of life.*
>
> *—Sense and Sensibility*

Dear Jane Austen,

I think my boyfriend is going to ask me to marry him. Great, right? Only, he makes very little money and I must confess that I like nice things—expensive things: fancy clothes, cars, vacation homes, French champagne, the best of everything. Another man, quite a bit older than me and my boyfriend (we're very young), has been pursuing me. He's very rich. I like him okay—he's nice to me and keeps promising me all the expensive things I love. I love my boyfriend but I mean this guy has mega-bucks. I know he would marry me and then even if it didn't work out and we divorced I would walk away with lots of money, maybe that summer house I dream about.

So, the romantic in me wants to stick with my penniless young boyfriend but the realistic side says, don't be a fool, get yourself set up now while you can command the best price and indulge in romance later. What do you think?

Prudent

~~&~~

Dear Prudent Heroine,

In responding to your question I shall have matter sufficient to fill this entire chapter. For the question of a heroine's attitude towards money and marriage has many facets, and I shall consider them each at length.

First, let me assure you that I am familiar with the lives led by those without a great deal of money, because for my entire life I have been such a person. I will not say I was poor, because I have never wanted for the necessities of life, but there has almost never been anything to spare for the luxuries. My father, a country parson, was driven to borrow heavily and take in pupils to make ends meet. It was trying, and worrying, to have a large family to launch into the world and few financial resources with which to do so, but we were certainly not harmed by living so modestly as children. But you have also heard the story of my father's sister, who found herself, naturally, without the same opportunities as her brother. Her determination to make a life for herself with no prospects led her to make the courageous voyage to India that resulted in a loveless marriage to a much older man. You are indeed fortunate that there is a less brutal divide between the sexes in your time, Prudent Heroine. *You* need not sell yourself, although your language of the marketplace would seem to indicate that you would not object to the analogy.

If a woman has the resolve and spirit of my Aunt Phila or, indeed, of my great-grandmother, Elizabeth Austen—you will recall that she became a schoolmistress after her husband died and thus successfully supported herself and her children—she need not have the same concerns about poverty as penniless women in my day, for her opportunities are far greater. A Jane Fairfax or my new novel's Clara Brereton, "who had been so low in every worldly view, as with all natural endowments and powers, to have

been preparing for a situation little better than a
nursery maid," would in your world be sure to rise
well above that station.

When you look in your heart, Prudent Heroine, do
you find that you share with my heroines the essential traits that would ensure their escape from poverty—should they happen to have been born into that
condition—if they lived in your meritocracy? No doubt
there will always be some women who lack the resources to make a good showing in life without un-
earned wealth. Such women must indeed follow a
different set of guidelines than those I set out for
women of heroine quality. They may not marry where
they choose. Mrs. Price, Fanny's mother, was such a
woman and chose a weak, negligent, vulgar man with
little money, and the results were disastrous:

> *Her disposition was naturally easy and indolent, like
> Lady Bertram's; and a situation of similar affluence
> and do-nothing-ness would have been much more
> suited to her capacity, than the exertions and self-
> denials of the one, which her imprudent marriage had
> placed her in. She might have made just as good a
> woman of consequence as Lady Bertram, but Mrs.
> Norris would have been a more respectable mother of
> nine children, on a small income.*

Such women as Mrs. Price and Lady Bertram must
marry for money, because they have not the character to keep themselves or raise their children respectably in a life of privation and hardship.

Very often wealth is a blessing bestowed on those
who are otherwise inferior or at best quite ordinary. It
gives them something to be vain about. But my heroines are certainly not impressed by wealth for its own
sake—though many other characters in my novels
are—and so I have an excellent contrast to place
before you between the correct and incorrect responses to money.

Even so good a person as Anne Elliot's friend Lady
Russell is blinded by rank and wealth; she disapproved of Anne's proposed marriage to the excellent

Captain Wentworth solely because he had not yet made any money, only to approve a future with the wicked William Walter Elliott almost entirely because he is her father's heir. Anne herself is unimpressed by wealth. She sees the insipidity, vanity, and heartless elegance of her father and elder sister clearly, and with disgust. She is appalled by the anxious solicitude they exhibit in attempting to renew their connection with noble cousins:

Anne was ashamed. Had Lady Dalrymple and her daughter even been very agreeable, she would still have been ashamed of the agitation they created, but they were nothing. There was no superiority of manner, accomplishment, or understanding.

Like a true, proud heroine, Elizabeth Bennet is similarly unimpressed with wealth:

She had heard nothing of Lady Catherine that spoke her awful from any extraordinary talents or miraculous virtue, and the mere stateliness of money and rank, she thought she could witness without trepidation.

Indeed, Lady Catherine is shown to be extremely ill-bred. And of course, Elizabeth rejects the first proposal of marriage by handsome, rich, supremely eligible Mr. Darcy despite his great wealth and her own very serious lack of a fortune.

Now, when Elizabeth comes to know Darcy better, after he has laboured to improve himself for her, she realizes that she was wrong in her judgment of him. But many a wealthy figure in my novels is shown to have no quality to recommend them besides wealth. The Bingley sisters have not much more than their fortunes to boast of, and Maria Bertram's rich fiancé is strongly disapproved of by her brother Edmund:

...no representation of his aunt's could induce him to find Mr. Rushworth a desirable companion. He could allow his sister to be the best judge of her own happiness, but he was not pleased that her happiness should centre in a large income; nor could he refrain from often saying to himself, in Mr. Rushworth's com-

*pany, "If this man had not twelve thousand a year, he
would be a very stupid fellow."*

Just as I am familiar with a life where there is
much hard work and little luxury (though in a style
certainly refined enough) I am also familiar with the
vastly different life of the very rich. My dear brother
Edward, as you know, was adopted by wealthy cousins and made their heir. He did not forget the rest of
his family and I—along with Cass, my parents, and
my other brothers—spent many nights in his splendid house, Godmersham. I lived then like a very fine
lady indeed. But I can assure you, many of those
days and nights were exceedingly dull. Some morn-
ings I sat in the library with five tables, eight and
twenty chairs and two fires all to myself. Edward's
fine neighbors called and came and sat and went and
there is no more to say about them. Now I adore
Edward, and his Fanny is like my own daughter; and
good Mrs. Knight, the standard for rich women eve-
rywhere—kind, wise, generous, my dear patroness.
But, as I have said elsewhere, to the company of the
local gentry I much preferred the company of the
governess, my cherished and clever friend Miss
Sharp.

And so, you hear quite my own opinion when Anne
Elliot corrects her cousin after he protests that the
noble Dalrymples are good company:

"My idea of good company, Mr. Elliot, is the company of clever, well-informed people, who have a great
deal of conversation; that is what I call good company."

To spending time in the superlatively stupid company of the merely rich, Anne much prefers to visit
with naval officers and their wives, who converse
eagerly on subjects of real interest, the Admiral's wife
"Mrs. Croft looking as intelligent and keen as any of
the officers around her." Although the Lyme home of
Captain Harville and his wife is extremely modest,
dinners there are so hospitably warm and lively—
being without any of the "formality and display" she

hates—that Anne is far more agreeably entertained there than in the luxurious rooms of the wealthy.

So you see that the filthy chaos in Fanny Price's childhood home—all dirt and confusion as it is—is not the result of the lack of money, but is a reflection of the characters of the presiding authorities, Mr. and Mrs. Price. You will protest that the harmony and cheerful orderliness, the peace and beauty of Mansfield Park are surely not unconnected with the enormous amount of money there, and I shall agree, adding only that those gifts of wealth indeed are nothing to those of its inhabitants who only appreciate "unmeaning Luxuries," as I once jokingly called them. Money does not make Maria and Julia good, Tom steady, Lady Bertram rational. It takes Fanny's sensitive nature, and that of her kindred spirit Edmund, to appreciate the blessings of money.

Did I say that harmony and beauty were the greatest gifts of wealth? I did not mean that. Without a doubt, the greatest gift of wealth is glorious independence...

Here is my brother Edward come to say good-bye. I do hope you leave your Fanny with us for a while longer. My sweet brother, what should my mother and Cass and I have done without your care? Look at these letters Fanny has brought me. It is to you my readers must be grateful, for in giving us Chawton Cottage to live in you restored me to tranquility. The fresh, clean air of the beautiful Hampshire countryside, the snug familiarity of my little daily routine: to these I owe the restoration of my ambition and my powers, both almost entirely stifled for the ten years we were unsettled. No wonder Fanny Price puts the highest value on an orderly home! Thank you, dear Edward. Take great care travelling on this wet, blowing day. Good-bye and my best love to my nieces and nephews at home. Tell little Cassandra-Jane that the pretty new tables also send their best love.

He is gone. Truly the best of brothers...and yet....
Do not, I beg you, take it as any mark of ingratitude,

Prudent Heroine, when I say that as much as I appreciate my brother's generous solicitude, I am unequal to a falsehood: I cannot but think what I have lost through having had no fortune of my own. I am the first to acknowledge that there is nothing superior about those who have wealth or position, and at least one of my heroines, Emma Woodhouse, must learn through painful lessons that she is wrong to rate them so highly that she is put off by Frank Churchill's "indifference to a confusion of rank" in the context of a friendly neighborhood ball. Sad to say, my darling Emma is a snob. But the rich do have one supreme advantage over the rest of us in the blessed power of independence, the freedom to do as they please. It is humiliating to think that for eight years I had not even the £10 necessary to buy *Northanger Abbey*—then called *Susan*, you know—back from the man who said he would publish it but never did. I have only just got *Miss Catherine*, as I now call this one of my darling children, back this year. Had I been in possession of my own fortune, I need not have bumped around Bath and Southampton, scarcely lifting a pen but to write letter to family and friends, for ten years. I can hardly hope to convey to you the difference in my life a small amount of my own money has made. What an increase in independence my modest earnings from my novels have given me!

But this logic will not do: for to imagine myself independent from birth is to imagine an entirely different life for myself. Had I been a woman of fortune, I would no doubt have been considered a fine match for Tom Lefroy, for it was surely our lack of money that prevented the marriage. We must have had something to live on besides love, and we had not. We did what was prudent, you see. And has it answered? Has it made us happy? I believe Mr. Irish Lefroy has got on very well and is prosperous in every way. And you see where I am. But no doubt you would prefer me to give examples from my novels, and I shall do so forthwith. I have no desire to fall into that sort of unreserve that is simply a vulgar familiarity.

"And to marry for money I think the wickedest thing in existence," says Catherine Morland; Emma Watson says, "Poverty is a great evil, but to a woman of education and feeling it ought not, it cannot be the greatest." The creator of these dear girls agrees with these sentiments, and yet I am wise and honest enough to give weight to good Elizabeth Watson's opposing view that she and her sister *must* marry because

"...it is very bad to grow old and be poor and laughed at." Prudent Heroine, you are very fortunate to have more alternatives than my heroines saw before them. You do not have to make this dreadful choice. Observe how things fall out for women in my novels—never my heroines, mind—who are driven by prudent—or mercenary—motives in matrimonial affairs.

You have heard Edmund Bertram's quite accurate assessment of his sister Maria's wealthy husband. Maria despised him and loved another, and married Mr. Rushworth for his wealth alone. The marriage certainly did not answer, and with nothing of affection, loyalty, or principle to prevent her from indulging her passion for Henry Crawford, she very soon found herself divorced by her husband, disappointed by her lover, and cast out of respectable society—something impossible to achieve in your time even with murder, so you need not fear that fate.

Mary Crawford, with a fortune of her own, has not the absolute need to marry a very rich man, yet she has determined on nothing less. She has the good taste to prefer Edmund Bertram to his elder brother, but is ultimately persuaded to accept the younger man's expected proposal only when she believes that Tom Bertram is at the point of death and that Edmund will become his father's heir. For all her attractions, Mary Crawford is mercenary and thus not suited to be a heroine, no matter how many readers believe otherwise.

145

Another who secured her own unhappiness by marrying badly is Mary Crawford's beautiful, lively young friend, Janet Fraser:

"She could not do otherwise than accept him, for he was rich, and she had nothing; but he turns out ill-tempered.... Poor Janet has been sadly taken in.... She took three days to consider of his proposals..."

Her taking but three days to consider marriage to a man for whom she feels no affection shows indeed that Janet Fraser felt she "could not do otherwise than accept him." But Edmund Bertram is less understanding of her situation than is her friend:

"She is a cold-hearted, vain woman, who has married entirely from convenience...the determined supporter of every thing mercenary and ambitious, provided it be only mercenary and ambitious enough."

You see, Prudent Heroine, I have little sympathy for characters who make choices from selfishness and vanity when those choices fail to result in their happiness.

Elizabeth Bennet's friend Charlotte Lucas felt similarly about Mr. Collins's proposal, although, portionless and never pretty, in her case she had not, to use your vulgar terms, the market value of Maria Bertram or Janet Fraser:

Without thinking highly either of men or of matrimony, marriage had always been her object; it was the only honorable provision for well-educated young women of small fortune, and however uncertain of giving happiness, must be their pleasantest preservative from want.

Although Elizabeth later sees how Charlotte contrives to make her marriage as little vexing as possible, she never truly reconciles herself to the fact that her good friend has sunk so low as to "[sacrifice] every better feeling to worldly advantage." Many women in my day, my Aunt Phila among them, have felt it necessary to make this bargain. As I have told your sister heroines-in-training, it was one I might have made myself, could I have brought myself to accept the hand of Harris Bigg-Wither. He was a friend and not at all a bad fellow, and I was very fond of his family. But a marriage without love? No, I could not have borne it, no more than Fanny Price could produce upon demand an affection for Henry Crawford, though the match appeared most eligible to all who cared about her. No doubt the same was thought of Harris's proposal to me.

I have no opinion of men who give too much consideration to a woman's fortune when choosing a wife either. Mr. Darcy's cousin Colonel Fitzwilliam tells Elizabeth Bennet that "Younger sons cannot marry where they like," to which she saucily replies, "Unless where they like women of fortune..." He clearly likes *her*—so clearly that she wonders if his remark is meant to be taken personally. But does it not appall you to see how unmanly a gentleman appears when he behaves in this mercenary fashion? For all the "spirit and flow" of Elizabeth's conversation with the Colonel, you know I would never see any of my heroines with a man who lets such concerns rule his behaviour and does not even scruple to admit it. Poor Elizabeth faces another such situation when her favourite, Colonel Wickham, leaves off his attentions to her in order to form an engagement with a new-made heiress. She coolly excuses his action by telling her aunt that "...handsome young men must have something to live on, as well as the plain," but my readers are not fooled by her rationalizing and know Mrs. Gardiner is right to disapprove of his actions. Later on, Elizabeth will see much of her past in a different light, and consider Wickham's designs on Mary King "the consequence of views solely and hatefully mercenary."

Willoughby also admits that his love for Marianne, and hers for him, were "insufficient to outweigh that dread of poverty, or get the better of those false ideas of the necessity of riches, which I was naturally inclined to feel, and expensive society had increased." So he cruelly spurns Marianne and marries a woman he does not love—the only "prudent" course for him. In speaking to Elinor, Willoughby calls the ideas that motivated him "false," but as she wisely points out to Marianne later, he regrets his actions only because they have not made him happy. Had he married Marianne and been poor, he would not have learned to embrace moderation and reject luxury, but would rather have resented her as the cause of his difficulties and soon ceased to love her, heartily regretting he had not married for money after all.

I told your sister heroines that I have written some lines of a new novel. You know it as *Sanditon,* but I dare say you have not read it, since it was never completed.... Well, never mind; we need not pursue that subject. Sir Edward, a character in this story, is another man who "*must* marry for money," and I confess, my prejudice against such men is once more apparent. Here is Charlotte Heyward's opinion of the handsome gentleman:

She began to think him downright silly...why he should talk so much nonsense, unless he could do no better, was un-intelligible. — He seemed very sentimental, very full of some feelings or other, and very much addicted to all the newest-fashioned hard words—had not a very clear brain she presumed, and talked a good deal by rote.

Upon my word, I cannot help it. Such men cannot have a right way of thinking, and I shall never be able to write of them as if they are anything close to the model of what a man should be.

In your time, and your country, men have more power in themselves. They are far better able to rise on their merits, and make their fates with their fortunes. They have the power to be men indeed, choosing women they like—and not such as will provide for them—as their wives. I would not have you be so foolish as to proclaim, with Isabella Thorpe, "Where people are really attached, poverty itself is wealth..." but rather consider if your young man has the prospect of a comfortable living in the future.

Prudent Heroine, do not you know how unhappy my darling Anne Elliot was made by allowing herself to be persuaded by Lady Russell to break her engagement to Captain Wentworth? For *he* was not forced by a lack of fortune to marry a woman he did not like merely for money. He had youth, health, courage, confidence. His future wealth was in his own hands. When I wrote of such men they were a newish breed, but I understand they are to be found in great numbers in your society. You cannot expect to have the same luck as Anne, who found herself in a position to reverse her decision eight years later, should your over-anxious caution about money lead you to make a similar error. (And you will take note that she was not gratifying any wish for wealth in breaking the engagement, but acting "principally for *his* advantage" in doing so.) But you might, like Anne, very much regret your choice when it fails to bring happiness, and in time you recognize how very mistaken you were:

She had been forced into prudence in her youth, she learned romance as she grew older—the natural sequel of an unnatural beginning.

If you would be a heroine, you will not risk your happiness by letting mercenary motives, disguised as prudence, lead you into marriage to a man you do not love.

> **JANE AUSTEN SAYS: A HEROINE DOES NOT MARRY FOR MONEY.**

I have not yet done. I fear I might have left you in some confusion about the value of prudence, for the same word is used to refer to somewhat different things, and like the word "pride" is liable to be misunderstood. Is not Elinor Dashwood the very picture of a prudent heroine, and do I not clearly approve of her attitude and behaviour? I shall begin to answer that question by giving you an illustration of miserliness masquerading as prudence in order to show you what prudence is not. (And by the bye, it is unfathomable to me how members of a family can allow money to destroy their mutual affection. That was not the case in the Austen family. Even my brother Henry's bankruptcy, which cost Edward tens of thousands of pounds, and many others of us our own little losses, was never held against him in the slightest degree. I am rather proud of that fact. There is nothing more abhorrent than rancour within a family caused by money.)

Is there anything more contemptible in all my novels than the meanness betrayed by Fanny and John Dashwood in the second chapter of *Sense and Sensibility*, in which a husband allows his wife to talk him out of giving his stepmother and half-sisters the financial help he promised his dying father he would give them—and this despite his being in a position to be generous? Fanny and John consider such selfishness *prudence*. Where it exists, you can be sure other unsavoury character traits flourish also, for excessive concern about money restricts the mind and heart. If a character is not entirely fiendish, he must continually rationalize, and delude himself, and think the worst of others, in order to continue to think well of himself. (Once again, how unlike what a man should be!) I shall place Elinor alongside her brother to allow you to see the difference between a laudable prudence and a despicable miserliness.

When Mrs. Dashwood, Elinor, and Marianne must remove from Norland, Mrs. Dashwood has some trouble finding a suitable dwelling for

...she could hear of no situation that at once answered her notions of comfort and ease, and suited the prudence of her eldest daughter, whose steadier judgment rejected several houses as too large for their income, which her mother would have approved.

Elinor is also successful in advising her mother to limit the number of servants in their new home, and to sell their carriage. Later she must convince Marianne to refuse Willoughby's present to her of a horse because they cannot afford to keep it. In this behaviour Elinor very much resembles Anne Elliot, the only member of her family to see the necessity of living within their reduced means, and to find shame rather than pride in a parade of the extravagance they can no longer afford. Anne proposes practical ways of retrenchment, guided by principles of honesty and justice in formulating these rigid requisitions, rather than consulting what is due to consequence and vanity. *This* sort of prudence is emphatically not the same as the prudence Anne renounces in favor of romance.

I shall conclude my letter by returning to everyone's favourite heroine: Elizabeth Bennet looked back in shame when she recalled how she was once so blind that she could ask: "Pray, my dear aunt, what is the difference in matrimonial affairs, between the mercenary and the prudent motive? Where does discretion end, and avarice begin?" For the sort of "prudence" that is so close to mercenariness as to be almost indistinguishable from it is not the sort to be found in—or countenanced by—any of my heroines. But the other sort of prudence, the kind possessed by Elinor and Anne, is the trait of a heroine and you, my dear, despite your signature, possess it not. Your love of luxury and ease betrays an *imprudence* that is distasteful in itself and is causing you to make extremely bad choices. I urge you to develop a proper sort of prudence so that you too will find the happiness that is the true heroine's portion.

I remain yours very sincerely,

Jane Austen

Chapter Ten
A Heroine's Happy Ending

The anxiety, which in this state of their at-
tachment must be the portion of Henry and
Catherine, and of all who loved either, as to
its final event, can hardly extend, I fear, to
the bosom of my readers, who will see in the
tell-tale compression of the pages before
them, that we are all hastening together to
perfect felicity.

—*Northanger Abbey*

Dear Would-be Heroine,

In the tell-tale compression of the pages before you,
you will see that my recommendations to you are
nearly at an end. You will by now understand—as I
pointed out to your sister, Studious Heroine—that an
essential element in the achievement of that perfect
felicity my heroines enjoy is the conquering of romantic illusions and expectations. Ah, does that seem to
you a contradiction? For what else is a heroine's
happy ending but precisely the embodiment of those
illusions and the fulfillment of the expectations? I do
not doubt that you misread my novels in this way, for
their stories have been very much perverted in the
retelling. As their source, allow me to clarify beyond
any doubt the truths they contain.

Unrealistic expectations, that is, those founded on
self-created delusions and not facts, are the enemy of
happy endings. Elizabeth Bennet's opinions and
prejudices, Emma Woodhouse's fanciful imaginings,

Catherine Morland's passionate belief in Gothic novels and Marianne's in romantic stories and poems all contribute to a false view of the world. The powerful emotion raised by Marianne's expectations—an ecstasy of hope—is not the happiness of security. No: "Marianne's joy was almost a degree beyond happiness, so great was the perturbation of her spirits..." As she waits without good cause for Willoughby's appearance,

Her spirits still continued very high, but there was a flutter in them which prevented their giving much pleasure to her sister, and this agitation increased as the evening drew on.

This agitation, the drama to which Marianne appears to be addicted, is not the felicity of a heroine's happy ending. My Heroines-in-Training, you must endeavour not to anticipate events except upon the strength of sober facts in order to avoid mirroring the endless cycle Marianne knows so well: "the anxiety of expectation and the pain of disappointment." The best way to ensure your success is to be content in the present reality and thus secure yourself against the need to imagine a magical happy ending that would remove you from daily boredom or dejection and fulfill a powerful yearning after romance and rescue by knights in shining armour.

For my heroines, the recognition of where their best hope of true happiness lies, can only come when their illusions about the world and about themselves are exposed for what they are. In such moments of truth the scales fall from their eyes and a sobering self-knowledge allows them to make decisions in love that are reasonable and realistic enough to give them a fair chance of living happily beyond the weddings that end my novels. Like Emma and Elizabeth, you will only recognize your true hero when you know yourself, and learn to see the world without the obscuring veil of self-created delusions.

Mr. Darcy defends his interference in Mr. Bingley's courtship of Jane Bennet by protesting that "[his]

investigations and decisions are not usually influenced by [his] hopes or fears," and whether or not his self-judgment is correct or, if correct, a sufficient excuse for his behaviour in this instance, the model he proposes is one I recommend for would-be heroines.

In the case of Fanny Price, it is the hero, Edmund Bertram, who must free himself of illusion, as he does when he acknowledges that the Mary Crawford he loved is not the real woman but—I quote him again—"the creature of [his] own imagination"—and that his ideal wife is a very different sort of woman.

Happy endings—good marriages—are the result of a clear vision of a spouse's character, for marriage is certainly not the stuff of romantic fancy. I return to a point I made earlier: nothing shows the brightness of my heroines' prospects for wedded bliss more than their unselfish concern for their heroes' welfare: Emma cannot bear to give Mr. Knightley pain, and will relieve him of it at any cost to herself, and he treats her with the same tender solicitude. He believes she loves Frank Churchill, and still wishes to comfort her; she encourages him to unburden his heart, though she is prepared to hear that it is full of love for another woman. I repeat, nothing in their story shows more the promise of a happy ending—not only on their wedding day but thirty or forty years hence—than this mutual tenderness, stronger and deeper than romantic passions that quickly flame up, and just as quickly expire. This scene shows also, as I explained to Timid Heroine, that it often happens that a heroine must take courageous action and speak boldly of her feelings to her hero—still saying no more than a lady should, of course—to let him know he need not despair. Thus does a heroine actively promote the enjoyment of her happy ending without compromising her feminine nature. I know how you hate passively waiting for what and whom you desire, though patience is often, very often, a woman's best suit.

Unrealistic expectations are one enemy of true and lasting happiness; another is prolonged indulgence in disappointment. The two are allies, both robbing a heroine's present of joy by keeping her preoccupied with future and past. We have seen various examples of the cruel delusions of false expectations; I shall now point out some instances of the other pitfall. You will notice that only my romantic heroines, Marianne and Anne, indulge in prolonged disappointment and regret. The others have moments when such feelings depress their spirits, certainly, but they do not dwell in them for long.

Elizabeth Bennet, as you well know, is "not formed for ill-humour," and though she is disappointed by Wickham's absence from the Netherfield ball, her spirits quickly rally. As her aunt says in comparing how she would have responded to being jilted to the way her sister Jane is reacting to Mr. Bingley's apparent retreat, "...you would have laughed yourself out of it sooner." And indeed, although Elizabeth indulges in some bitter sarcasm ("Stupid men are the only ones worth knowing, after all"), thereby revealing her disappointment in the loss of Wickham's attention, she is diverted at once by her aunt's invitation to join her and her husband on a tour of pleasure to the Lakes, and eagerly enters into the plan. Even after she reads Mr. Darcy's letter and learns the shocking truth about Wickham's character, her wit is soon spirited enough to make Jane say, "Lizzy, when you first read that letter, I am sure you could not treat the matter as you do now." Although Elizabeth likes Darcy's cousin, Colonel Fitzwilliam, very much, he "had made it clear that he had no intentions at all, and...she did not mean to be unhappy about him." And, as one last example of a heroine's resilience, I remind you of how Elizabeth dismisses the anxious uncertainty she feels about Darcy's intentions: "If he is satisfied with only regretting me, when he might have obtained my affections and hand, I shall soon cease to regret him at all." Elizabeth is blessed with a naturally happy temper, but you see how she assists it by not dwelling on disappointments, even if that involves persuading herself as well as another that she has not been wounded.

Now, Catherine Morland is listless and unhappy when she returns from Bath, which, for a girl of seventeen just parted from her first lover, perhaps forever, is quite natural. Catherine is by nature a sensible girl, but there are some situations of the human mind in which good sense has very little power, and she must be allowed a period of disappointment given what she has suffered. But my readers know she would recover in time and not sink into a permanent state of dejection over Henry Tilney even if he should never return. Catherine is no Marianne, courting misery, nourishing grief, and convinced of the impossibility of second attachments, and she has heretofore shown the elasticity of her spirit (as well as her walk) on many occasions. Indeed, Marianne herself is no Marianne on this score, as we discover.

Marianne's most cherished maxim is that "no one can ever be in love more than once in their life." Her sister Elinor disagrees:

"...after all that is bewitching in the idea of a single and constant attachment, and all that can be said of one's happiness depending entirely on any particular person, it is not meant—it is not fit—it is not possible that it should be so."

And yet it is this very conviction that causes Marianne and so many would-be heroines today so much anguish when their great romances end—a conviction to which they cleave even in spite of their own experience to the contrary. (I believe the term used in describing these unique lovers is "soulmates.") But it is no creed of mine that such disappointments kill anyone. Elinor is right, as her sister ultimately recognizes, acknowledging that she could never have been happy with Willoughby even if he had kept faith with her. Marianne's happy ending was not dependent upon him after all. In time she marries and falls in love with Colonel Brandon, a much better man.

I must commend my Marianne for changing in response to experience, for without such a capacity for learning and improving she would not be a heroine. Notice how many women in my novels never change, but remain rigidly fixed in their ways, often strictly confined in their conversation and occupation to one or two subjects, without alteration or addition. But my *heroines* are never so limited in their speech or their views, though as women they are perforce constricted in their movements as men are not.

My brother Henry has returned again to inform me that the storm has quieted to a mere mizzle, almost a nothing. Ah, but he has more important matters than the skies to lecture me about. He asks if I believe Marianne could truly have fallen as passionately in love with Brandon as she once was with Willoughby, and he informs me that not one of my readers believes such a thing and moreover, that neither does Elinor. He says I have forgotten that after hearing Willoughby's *apologia* Elinor "doubted whether... [Marianne] could ever be happy with another; and for a moment wished Willoughby a widower."

I remind my dear brother that it was impossible for Marianne to be tolerably happy with Willoughby in reality, given the truth of his character. That was a romantic dream that could not survive the light of day. Elinor quickly realizes this truth. I must insist again that Marianne would have been miserable married to him. To imagine a happy ending there is to imagine what could never be—and that is precisely the bad habit I am trying to help my heroines-in-training break. I implore him not to encourage you with false hopes! My brother takes my pen out of my hand and writes to you directly.

You are cruel, Jane. You mock your poor heroine for imagining herself doomed to lament forever the loss of Willoughby, "remaining even for ever with her mother, and finding her only pleasures in retirement and study," as if such a fate were unheard of except in romance, and yet we do see it in life amongst those who have lost their first loves—their Knightleys in shining armour, we might say, if we suspected you of sly, subterranean romanticism.

Hush, Henry, you get upon delicate subjects. No doubt you refer to our dear Cass, only twenty-four when her Tom died, and never to look at another man in that way again. So very sad, to be widowed before being married. But Cass is an Austen, and she behaved with resolution and propriety under the most trying of circumstances. She did not make her family suffer any more than we would have in any case. But I should have been happy—indeed I should—to see her rally and form a second attachment, and to find her beautiful face reproduced in the faces of two or three nieces.

But to be sure, Jane, such disappointments do not kill anyone. And I was not thinking of Cass only...

I am determined not to allow my brother further use of my pen. He presses too hard with it and will render it useless. I shall respond to his insolence and so have the last word.

They did not kill me, if that is what you mean. Some dreams must die for others to live, and my children—my novels, you know—have brought me as much joy as anyone has a right to expect. My life has been quite happy. Heroines-in-training must accept the necessity of compromise if they are to be happy in real life. Perfect happiness is found only in novels. I fear you have been studying them, Henry. Where else would you have learned this unmeaning gibberish? No, I certainly will not lend you my pen again, for I tremble at the thought of your influence on my heroines-in-training.

Willoughby compromises, and his fate is not entirely unhappy. Although he would have preferred Marianne if she came with a large fortune, he survives well enough in his choice of a less amiable but wealthy woman:

...that he was for ever inconsolable, that he fled from society, or contracted an habitual gloom of temper, or died of a broken heart, must not be depended on—for

*he did neither. He lived to exert, and frequently to
enjoy himself. His wife was not always out of humour,
nor his home always uncomfortable; and in his breed
of horses and dogs, and in sporting of every kind, he
found no inconsiderable degree of domestic felicity.*

A strange creature by way of a soulmate, to be so
easily consoled!

Another gentleman who loses a woman he loves—
through no fault of his own—is Captain Benwick,
whose fiancée Fanny Harville died while he was at
sea. He is deeply afflicted by the loss, and believes he
will never get over it. As I reminded you earlier, in a
kindhearted effort to help rouse him out of his melancholy state, Anne Elliot urges him to read more
prose and less romantic poetry, a pastime that only
increases his melancholy. As in Marianne's case,
there is an element of dramatic intensity in his situation that he finds compelling in spite—or because—of
its anguish. Thus, when Anne speaks to him of it, his
looks show him "not pained, but pleased with this
allusion to his situation." As she predicts, Benwick
rallies, and before too long a period of mourning is
engaged to Louisa Musgrove, whom he has kept
company during the period of her convalescence.
Another instance of a man's extraordinary failure to
die of a broken heart! (Catherine Morland, as you
know, "read all such works as heroines must read to
supply their memories with those quotations which
are so serviceable and so soothing in the vicissitudes
of their eventful lives," and it is to Shakespeare's
Rosalind that heroines must look for the apt line
here: "...men have died from time to time, and worms
have eaten them, but not for love.")

Anne speaks for all women (in these lines that did
not exist this morning) when she says to Fanny's
brother, Captain Harville, "We certainly do not forget
you, so soon as you forget us." That is a sad and
poignant truth, and yet...I can also see the comedy in
woman's habit of holding on to a love that is impossible to consummate for one reason or another, particularly when the "love" is more truly on the order of

infatuation, and the feeling is not returned. Although it is incomprehensible to Emma that a woman could persist in an unrequited affection, Harriet Smith appears incapable of striving against her attachment to the now-married Mr. Elton, and reason good:

> *The charm of an object to occupy the many vacancies of Harriet's mind was not to be talked away. He might be superseded by another; he certainly would indeed; nothing could be clearer; even a Robert Martin would have been sufficient; but nothing else, she feared, would cure her. Harriet was one of those, who, having once begun, would be always in love.*

(Lydia Bennet resembles Harriet in this, with affections "continually fluctuating, but never without an object." She too, as Elizabeth says, feeds her dangerous romantic inclinations: "She has been doing every thing in her power by thinking and talking on the subject, to give greater...susceptibility to her feelings...") And I believe there are few moments in my novels more amusing than the revelation to Emma of Harriet's box of "Most Precious Treasures," filled with little bits of junk she has been saving because Mr. Elton touched them, only taking the box out and looking at its contents "now and then as a great treat." And yet, Marianne bears some resemblance to Harriet in her complete surrender to feelings of hopeless love. Both girls exhibit perverse, compulsive behaviour, designed only to increase wretchedness. Could Emma's lecture to her little friend on the subject not just as well come from Elinor? Emma asks Harriet to exert herself:

> "for the sake of what is more important than my comfort, a habit of self-command in you, a consideration of what is your duty, an attention to propriety, an endeavour to avoid the suspicions of others, to save your health and credit, and restore your tranquility."

And Harriet's being in love with three men in one year, and feeling the same degree of painfully stimulating attachment each time, is merely an accelerated version of the thankfully comic truth I illustrate in various places: that eternal constancy to a lost love is to be found far more frequently in literature than in life. Do not emulate Harriet—she is no model for a heroine.

And so, my endings frequently celebrate—with wry wit, if I may say so—the blessed resiliency of the human heart. Of Lady Susan's lover and daughter I wrote when I was very young:

Frederica was therefore fixed in the family of her uncle and aunt, till such time as Reginald De Courcy could be talked, flattered and finessed into an affection for her—which, allowing leisure for the conquest of his attachment to her mother, for his abjuring all future attachments and detesting the sex, might be reasonably looked for in the course of a twelvemonth. Three months might have done it in general, but Reginald's feelings were no less lasting than lively.

Edmund Bertram says of Mary Crawford, "I cannot give her up, Fanny. She is the only woman in the world whom I could ever think of as a wife." Even after he *has* given her up, and is aware that his brother's severe illness had enlivened her interest in him as the next heir, he believes his disappointment and suffering will continue only a little abated, and that "...still it was a sort of thing which he never could get entirely the better of...." But Edmund is no more a tragic torch-carrier than most mortals, and so I wrote:

I purposely abstain from dates on this occasion, that every one may be at liberty to fix their own, aware that the cure of unconquerable passions, and the transfer of unchanging attachments, must vary much as to time in different people.—I only entreat every body to believe that exactly at the time when it was quite natural that it should be so, and not a week earlier, Edmund did cease to care about Miss Crawford, and became as anxious to marry Fanny, as Fanny herself could desire.

You will recall that I also acknowledged that had Henry Crawford persisted in his pursuit of Fanny, he would have won her affection and her hand, in the transfer of yet another unchanging attachment.... I am pleased to inform you that my brother is content now I have confessed once again that his namesake would have triumphed. He leaves us in peace.

Good-night, dearest brother.

It is true that the admirable Anne Elliot harbours a love for a man she does not see for almost eight years, and while she is, in her selflessness, the antithesis of her sister in romanticism, Marianne, she is nonetheless an example of how such extreme romanticism can ruin a life. Although in my story Frederick Wentworth does return after so many years with his love undimmed, in real life this is a most unlikely event, and I am not necessarily recommending that you follow Anne's example. I confess to a rare indulgence in romantic fancy myself in this instance, and the powerful appeal of such dreams is evident: no other pair of lovers in all my writing has a sweeter ending. But there is also this striking difference between Anne and you, my dear readers: Anne lived a Regency woman's life of limited mobility and opportunity, which you do not. You are far luckier than she is in that respect. You will recall my rational explanation for the persistence of her love:

...she had been too dependant on time alone; no aid had been given in change of place...or in any novelty or enlargement of society.—No one had ever come within the Kellynch circle, who could bear a comparison with Frederick Wentworth, as he stood in her memory. No second attachment, the only thoroughly natural, happy, and sufficient cure, at her time of life, had been possible to the nice tone of her mind, the fastidiousness of her taste, in the small limits of the society around them.

You do not live within the same confined sphere. In her limited circle, she never saw his equal—but in all the world, which is *your* domain? I shall treat you to some more of the dialogue I mean to include in my revision. Here is Anne, again speaking to Captain Harville on behalf of all women:

"We live at home, quiet, confined, and our feelings prey upon us. You are forced on exertion. You have always a profession, pursuits, business of some sort or other, to take you back into the world immediately, and continual occupation and change soon weaken impressions."

Anne loves the man, to be sure, but she also sees him as her escape from the coldness and tedium of home into a life of travel, adventure, novelty; moreover into a society she finds warm, exciting, and interesting—in short, a life the very antithesis of the one she was born into. You, dear Would-be Heroine, have the opportunity to meet countless numbers of men, and you do not in any case *need* one to find the society or the occupation you desire. Still, most women in your day, living without the limitations of my heroines, nonetheless make the error of relying too heavily on men for their happiness and so prevent or delay their own cure.

I must be sure to remind Cass to take care that no letters of mine are left to betray any such foolish inclinations of my own, for I shall not outlive my elder sister. I should not like to give the incorrect impression that any such romantic notions unduly influenced the course of my life. And yet, Would-be Heroine, the event is already determined; you and I both know that some sentences of mine *have* escaped the fire. What they reveal, they reveal.

Fanny, my dear, have you come to say good-night? It gives me great joy to learn that you are spending the night at Chawton Cottage. Anna stays too? My two favourite nieces, how delightful. Do bid good-night to all for me. I am afraid I am too tired to go downstairs again. Yes, it is true that I have borne the arrival of these letters extremely well. Anybody might have thought they were giving me pleasure, and for that I thank you. There, I have made you smile once again. My love, you have indeed been one of the great joys of my life, as dear to me as any daughter. Always remember your Aunt Jane at her most agreeable, I beseech you, and forget entirely my moments of spleen. Oh, nothing, nothing to be concerned about. I daresay you know my little freaks well enough by now. I mean just nothing at all—do not look so sad. Good-night, dearest Fanny.

Dear Would-be Heroine, my most romantic hero- ines, the girls with the most sensitive natures—surely you have noticed that these are the ones who are the least lively and gay. Elinor describes Marianne as "not often really merry." To be sure, I know about that painful side of life and love, as who does not? But we need not therefore cultivate it amongst hero- ines. I should rather see my heroines-in-training performing in comedies, not tragedies. And so I urge you to choose happiness, my dear. Comedy admits the necessity of compromise and accommodation in love. But the compromise women must make is only with the romantic fancy, and therefore very little of true value is lost when, at story's end, we see such amusing contrasts between the plans and decisions of mortals as time is for ever producing. My heroines have happy endings because their marriages are founded on reality, not fancy. Romance with delusion as its foundation will rather end in tragedy, or a sad something far too ignoble to deserve the name.

Poor Cass. She did not have my consolations....

I beg your pardon if I have anywhere in my letters lapsed into precept. As I have said, I mean only to put before you the consequences of certain choices—the choices themselves are entirely up to you.

Our correspondence, to the great detriment of the Post Office revenue, is at an end for this day. I sus- pect tomorrow's post will lure dear Fanny into the muddy lanes once again, and she will return with her arms full of new solicitations for me. Well, like Lady Catherine, I love to be of use; depend upon it, I shall happily advise every heroine-in-training who seeks my counsel. Pray forgive me too, Would-be Heroine, if

164

I have been eloquent on points in which my own conduct ill bears examination.

The skies have cleared and it is a fine moonlight night. Cassandra will reappear in a moment, I have no doubt, and we shall have a comfortable coze by the fire, and then to bed. The next thing we know, the cock will be crowing. Yes, all my Would-be Heroines, some dear, tender dreams must fade away with the moonlight but would not you rather laugh in the sunshine and sweet air of the fine waking world? ...Another very pretty, perfectly nonsensical analogy! It will never do. Such flowery phrases will lead my heroine-readers astray, and there are stories enough to do that. I promise to abjure such language forever, and return to you in the morning as cool and clever as Elizabeth Bennet. Adieu. With best love, &c., I remain

Yours affectionately,

Jane Austen

~~&~~

The calls of Canadian geese woke me from a deep slumber. The light still burned on my bedside table, illuminating the cover of *Persuasion* that lay beneath it. The time displayed on the clock-radio told me it would be dark outside for a little while longer. I could hear the low melancholy roar of the surf accompanying the sharp cries of the flock as it flew south. Winter was coming. I was about to spend my last morning in this house where I'd been holed up for two weeks. My self-imposed exile was over. Time to pack up my Jane Austen novels and self-help books, all brought here in the hope they could heal my heart, give me relief from the pain of—what else?—a love affair gone south.

What a dream I had! I chuckled as I collected the books and carted them downstairs, thinking of Jane Austen dispensing advice on Internet dating and cell-phone etiquette. Dear Would-Be Heroine indeed.

I thought I would have breakfast on the road rather than linger here any longer. Tea and scones and clotted cream?

More like Denny's Grand Slam. I think that's what Elizabeth Bennet would order to keep those heroine fires stoked. It was time to go. I packed up my contact lens solutions and wool sweaters. I loaded my belongings into the trunk. The fog had burned away and the sun was quickly rising over the Atlantic. Back in the city I would miss these sounds, that smell. But I had had enough of solitude. I wanted to be around people again.

I hadn't checked my e-mail or phone messages for two weeks. I gave this number to no one. If he hadn't written or called I didn't want to know until I reached home. I was sure he had, though. I know he missed me. He loved me, after all.

Foolish girl! Remember what Jane Austen says: a heroine—what was it? A heroine founds her expectations on facts and common sense, not fantasy! A heroine loves romantic stories but does not mistake them for life!

I slid behind the wheel and then remembered I had left my notebook upstairs, on the desk in the bedroom. My precious notebook, full of advice carefully copied out each night, advice for women like me, who love too much, give too much, suffer too much—and think too little! Women who let voluntary, self-created delusions ruin their happiness. I ran back into the house, taking a last glance around for anything else I might have left behind. I had learned a few things from the books about living in the real world instead of in dreams and I was ready to go back and start again, alone if I had to. To be the heroine of my own life, whether he had called or not.

Why hold out false hope? Alone. But I shall soon cease to regret him at all.

I ran up the stairs and into the bedroom, now beginning to brighten with daylight. As I snatched my notebook from the desk I stopped. My eyes must have been playing tricks on me, I thought, and squinted hard. Was it only the creative eye of fancy that still saw there—on a desk in a seaside cottage in New Jersey, in the year 2005—a quill pen, the tip still wet and gleaming in the morning light?

Finis

Printed in the United States
46678LVS00002B/20